Science Is Golden

Science Is Golden

A Problem-Solving Approach to Doing Science with Children

Ann Finkelstein

Michigan State University Press • *East Lansing*

∞ The paper used in this publication meets the minimum requirements
of ANSI/NISO Z39.48–1992 (R 1997) (Permanence of Paper).

Michigan State University Press
East Lansing, Michigan 48823-5202

Printed and bound in China

07 06 05 04 03 02 01   1 2 3 4 5 6 7 8 9 10

LIBRARY OF CONGRESS CATALOGING-IN-PUBLICATION DATA
Finkelstein, Ann.
Science is golden: a problem-solving approach to doing science
with children / Ann Finkelstein.
p. cm.
Includes bibliographical references.
ISBN 0-87013-566-X (pbk. : alk. paper)
1. Science—Study and teaching (Elementary)—Activity programs.
2. Problem-based learning. I. Title.
LB1585 .F54 2001
372.3'5—dc21
2001004689

Cover design by Heidi Dailey
Book design by Sharp Des!gns, Lansing, MI
Illustration by Barbara Hranilovich

_____

Visit Michigan State University Press on the World Wide Web at:
www.msu.edu/unit/msupress

to Sam and Jeremy

CONTENTS

FIGURES *&* TABLES

ACKNOWLEDGMENTS

MY HUSBAND, ZACHARY BURTON, FIRST SUGGESTED THAT I WRITE THIS BOOK. His encouragement, editing, and helpful suggestions made its completion possible. The curiosity of our sons, Samuel and Jeremy Burton, is an ongoing inspiration for me. I thank them for their many scientific questions and for their help in performing experiments. I thank my mother, Verna Finkelstein, for enthusiastically supporting this project.

Most of the children's scientific questions used in this book were collected from students at Wilkshire Early Childhood Center and Vera Rayla Elementary School in Haslett, Michigan. Principals Sherren Jones and Patti Lutzke graciously agreed to let me collect questions from their students. I appreciate the efforts of the teachers who handed out and collected the fliers containing the scientific questions. I am most indebted to the children who asked (and wrote down) their scientific questions. I hope their wonderful curiosity remains with them throughout their lives.

I thank Elizabeth Ternes for letting me help her with her fourth-grade science project, and for donating the data from the sledding experiment to this book. I also thank the Ternes family for their encouragement and advice.

Carol Amor kindly allowed me to do science experiments with her first grade class at Wilkshire Early Childhood Center. I appreciate her generosity in letting me test my theories in her classroom. Her students' creative suggestions for keeping air away from apple slices are discussed in Chapters 3 and 7.

I thank Phyllis DeGioia and Judith Katsh for their careful reading of this manuscript. Their thoughtful suggestions helped make this book more user-friendly.

The electron micrograph of HIV-1 in Chapter 2 is the generous gift of Dr. Robert F. Garry, Professor of the Department of Microbiology and Immunology at Tulane University Medical Center.

I thank Dr. Michele Fluck, distinguished professor of the Department of Microbiology at Michigan State University for reading this manuscript and sending it to Dr. Bruce Alberts, president of the National Academy of Sciences. I also thank Dr. Bruce Alberts for finding the time to read my book and offering encouragement and suggestions. I count Dr. Alberts's kind words among the high points of my career.

Lei Lei, Stephan Reimers, Delin Ren, Kevin Carr, and Kaillathe Padmanabhan provided computer assistance. Lei Lei, Yong Wong, and their many Internet friends translated the proverb at the beginning of Chapter 1 back into Chinese. Sara Katsh helped with referencing. Tony Sills explained how the television remote control works, and suggested some experiments. Steven Johnson told me how apple cider is made.

I thank the two anonymous reviewers for their compliments and suggestions.

Finally, I thank Martha A. Bates at Michigan State University Press for believing in this book.

INTRODUCTION

THE INSPIRATION FOR WRITING THIS BOOK WAS MY CHILDREN'S CURIOSITY. AS I helped them explore their scientific interests, I was struck by how much children are like scientists. They seem to have an insatiable curiosity, they love to investigate unfamiliar concepts and objects, and they analyze what they observe. The motivation for writing this book was the opportunity to help a neighbor, Lizzy, with her fourth grade science project. I was impressed by her knowledge base and organizational abilities, and I wanted to direct Lizzy to a book that would help her plan, perform, and analyze her own experiment. I was disappointed to find only information on pre-designed experiments. It occurred to me that children have most of the skills required to investigate their own scientific questions, but they need some help in developing these skills. There should be more information available about how to create experiments. I wanted this book to be that kind of resource. Lizzy's experiment that compares the relative speed of sleds on a snow-covered hill is frequently used as an example.

One evening during the planning stages of Lizzy's experiment, her mother called me to ask a few questions about experimental design. Lizzy's younger sister, Marie, asked, "Mom, are you calling the Magic School Bus?" Her mom answered, "No. The next best thing." I have not dyed my hair red, and I generally refrain from wearing *very* unusual clothes, but I was honored to be compared to Ms. Frizzle. I hope this book will be the "next best thing" to having a friendly scientist on the phone to help plan, perform, and analyze children's experiments.

In this book I offer advice for adults who wish to help children investigate their own scientific questions. The process starts with children's curiosity. By analyzing their ideas, and employing problem-solving techniques, young children can, with help, invent their own scientific experiments. This "do it yourself" method may reduce the misgivings some students, teachers, and parents have about science.

Science Is Golden

1 The Brains-On Approach

to Science

聞而忘　　*What I hear I forget.*
視而記　　*What I see I remember.*
行而知　　*What I do I understand.*
　　　　　　　　　　—*Chinese proverb*

Science is not just for nerds.

Science is often perceived as a boring subject, although I cannot understand why. Science is the study of life and death, the oceans and the earth, the flora and the fauna. Science investigates the smallest particles of matter and the breadth of the universe. Science explains why Michael Jordan can jump so high, and just how difficult it is to hit a knuckle ball. Scientific research has developed technologies to allow astronauts to survive in outer space. Science holds the answers to why our children may look like us, or why they may not. The study of science has yielded the cure or prevention for horrible diseases. Science can help us determine ways to keep this planet a safe and beautiful place for many generations to come. What is boring about that?

Science is an extremely creative subject, and yet the creative aspects of science are often overlooked. Many people apply the word "creative" to art, music, dance, poetry, and fiction, rather than to science. Finding the solution to any problem, whether it is how to paint a landscape or how to map the path of a comet requires creative thought. Creative problem solving requires two steps. First, the solution to the problem must be imagined. The landscape must be envisioned by the artist, or the elliptical orbit of the comet must be hypothesized by the astronomer. The second creative process is imagining unique ways to solve the problem. The artist finds a new and different way to portray the scene, while the astronomer uses the comet's previous locations to predict how it moves through space. Scientific thought is organized by formal problem-solving techniques. Logical thinking no more limits the creative aspects of science than the methods for applying paint to canvas limit the creativity of artists. Without creative thought, there would be few scientific advances.

Science is on the brink of countless amazing and wonderful discoveries, and the media has sensationalized some recent breakthroughs. The famous sheep, Dolly, was "cloned" by fusing a mammary cell to an unfertilized, DNA-free egg.[1] Dolly's exis-

tence caused public outcry and discussions of the moral implications of this new technology. While several kinds of animals have been cloned successfully, human cloning remains technically difficult, impractical, and less efficient than traditional methods. Popular fiction often portrays scientists as the bad guys planning nefarious plots with evil purposes. Let me try to reassure you here. Scientific research is very carefully regulated. The use of chemicals, radioisotopes, animals, recombinant DNA technology, and human tissues is closely monitored. Laboratories that fail to comply with these regulations are not allowed to continue operating. We tend to fear things we do not understand, but science is not incomprehensible, and it need not be feared. Showing children how to plan experiments and analyze data will prepare them to understand and scrutinize future scientific developments. Establishing a positive attitude about science allows children to examine technological advances logically without anxiety coloring their thoughts.

Science *is* a difficult subject. Professional scientists investigate some of the most interesting, challenging, and important problems that the world has ever known. Science, however, can be done at many levels. Children can learn to appreciate the beauty of analytical thought, the perfection of nature, and the thrill of investigation without being intimidated by complicated details. There is plenty of time for them to learn about the Higg's boson, should they so desire. Now is the time to communicate that science is fun, understandable, useful, and interesting. You don't have to be a rocket scientist to do experiments. All you need is an open mind and the desire to solve problems. Nearly all of the references I have used in the preparation of this book can be found in the children's section of the public library. Research will undoubtedly be required, but it isn't necessary to wade through a graduate-level physics book to help design an experiment to answer "How does a kite fly?"

Science is based on logical arguments and simple strategies. The laws of nature govern everything from the smallest subatomic particles to the movement of the planets. There are relatively few scientific principles, and most of them can be understood in a way that is simple and intuitive. The key to much of biology is the survival of the fittest, and the need for animals to develop a niche where they can live, eat, and reproduce. Perhaps more natural laws govern the physical world, but there are many interesting systems that can be presented in a user-friendly way. Two of the questions I collected from a fifth grade student illustrate this concept: "Why are baby animals so cute?" and "How does a musical instrument make sound?"

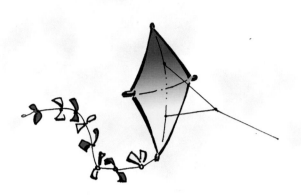

While several complex scientific concepts are involved in flying a kite, the main reason is simple. *The wind pushes it up.* The pressure of the wind against the inclined surface of the kite generates lift. We have all experienced Newton's third law of motion: "To every action, there is an equal and opposite reaction." In this case, the action of the wind when it is deflected downward off the flat surface of the kite causes a reaction of the kite getting pushed up. The angle of the kite against the wind is important. The kite strings maintain the appropriate angle.[2] Think of all the experiments that could be done investigating the shape, size, weight, construction materials, and steering capabilities of a kite.

First, how do Darwin's theories apply to baby animals? Cuteness has survival benefits. Soft fur or downy feathers keep small animals or birds warm. The spots on a fawn act as camouflage when the baby hides from predators, and the long legs on a zebra foal enable it to run with the herd shortly after birth. When young animals play, they are developing important survival skills such as running or hunting.[3] Of course, the details of a biological system may have to be researched, but the underlying concept of the need to survive puts many details into perspective.

Similarly, young children can design experiments to investigate how a musical instrument makes sound by examining the ideas of vibration and sound waves. When we hear sound, we perceive vibrations. These vibrations move through the air as sound waves, which are detected by our ears. Slower vibrations make lower sounds; faster vibrations make higher pitches.[4] This is fertile ground for designing experiments. Noise-making vibrations can be produced by twanging stretched rubber bands, tapping bottles filled with different amounts of water, rubbing a moistened finger around the rim of a stemmed glass, ringing bells, etc.

Science is further simplified by the use of controlled experiments. If an experiment is properly planned, it should yield data that are easy to analyze. The results of a controlled experiment should point to the correct answer. Here is an example. The children in a first-grade soccer league wear reversible blue and gold T-shirts. Each team is assigned a color for each game, and players on opposing teams are differentiated by the color of their shirts. The teams switch colors from week to week.

After the first three games, one boy wondered, "Why does the blue team always win?" Adults realize that these results are simple coincidence. Eliminating misleading chance occurrences in scientific experiments is important, however. The best way to avoid being deceived is to do controlled experiments. How can the "blue team theory" be tested? The simplest experiment would involve only two teams. The teams should play soccer six or eight times. (The large number of games helps "average out" day-to-day variations in the level of play.) As all players will probably improve their soccer skills over the course of the experiment, each team should wear the coveted blue T-shirt for alternate games. I suspect that by the end of the experiment, there would be no correlation between winning and the color of the jersey. If all the players believed that the blue shirt conferred good luck, it is possible that the added self-confidence would affect the outcome of the game. The best experiment would involve players who did not know that the "blue team theory" was being tested. (Note added in proof: the gold team won the fourth and fifth games.) If the experiment is bounded by controls, it is easier to draw correct conclusions from the data. (Designing controlled experiments is explained more completely in Chapter 4.)

Young children can be introduced to science in a variety of ways. In this book, I propose a method that starts with children's questions about science. Students then design experiments to answer their questions, and learn how to analyze and present their data. I favor this technique because the "Brains-On Method" is a complete representation of the scientific method, and because students are likely to feel responsible for and interested in experiments of their own creation. The brains-on method is just one approach to teaching science, but the techniques described in this book can also be used to enhance and clarify other methods. All students should be encouraged to ask questions. Experimental controls can be added to science demonstrations. The suggestions for graphing, preparing laboratory notebooks, and creating posters can be applied to any experiment. Most importantly, children should have a personal stake in the experiment. Children are naturally curious, and science is a way they can learn about their world. To use the words of Dr. Bruce Alberts, president of the National Academy of Sciences, "learning science is something that students do, not something that is done to them."

The brains-on approach helps students create their own experiments.

The brains-on method goes one step beyond hands-on science activities for children. Not only do the students do the experiment, they first conceive of the idea, refine their idea, plan the experiment, perform a controlled experiment, and analyze and present the results. This is easier than it seems. It does not require trained professionals, and you can attempt it in your own home or classroom. Here is a brief overview of the brains-on approach to science.

❶ *Start with science questions asked by children.*
The world around, above, below, and within us is fascinating, and children are naturally curious about themselves and their environment. I tried to tap into that curiosity by collecting questions from elementary school students. As a scientist, I was delighted with the quality of the questions and gratified to know the answers to some of them. The questions varied in subject, scope, and difficulty. Some were easily answered. "How many grams are in a pound?" (There are about 454 g/lb.) Some questions hint at problems of such importance that their answer may someday be worthy of a Nobel Prize. "How does medicine know where to go?" (The efforts of many talented scientists and many research dollars are currently being directed at "magic bullet" therapies in which anti-cancer drugs are targeted directly at the cancerous tissue.) By starting with questions asked *by* students, we start with their interest, and show them how to follow up on it.

❷ *Show how students can turn questions into experiments.*

Chapter 2 is about questions. Several examples are given of how questions can be clarified and refined so that they can serve as the nucleus of an experiment. Of course, not every question leads to an experiment, but if enough questions are collected, there are sure to be some that are suitable for experimentation. How to turn a clear and well-thought out question into an experiment is discussed in Chapter 3. With some adult guidance, a group of children can work together to build a model of how they think their experimental system may work. They propose possible answers to their question, and think of ways to test which of their ideas are correct.

❸ *Plan the experiment.*

In Chapter 4, I explain how to do a controlled experiment. Experimental controls are often overlooked in elementary science, but controls make the results more meaningful. Controls frame the logical argument. Negative controls measure background, and positive controls test if the experiment is working. Many examples of negative and positive controls are presented as well as reasons for doing them.

❹ *Do the experiment.*

Doing the experiment and collecting the data are two of the most fun parts of the experimental process. Data must be collected in an organized and careful manner. Chapter 5 covers doing the experiment, collecting the data, and keeping a laboratory notebook.

❺ *Figure out what was learned.*

How to make sense out of the data is discussed in Chapter 6. Lots of numbers can be baffling. Non-numeric data can be confusing too. Making sense of the experimental results and understanding the data is fun and rewarding. Topics include graphing, experimental error, qualitative analysis, and presentation of data. These subjects are discussed in a way that is appropriate for experiments done by young children.

❻ *Ask more questions.*

Did the results of the experiment lead to more questions? Is it possible to follow up on any of these questions? How could the experiment be improved? Was something unexpected learned from the experiment?

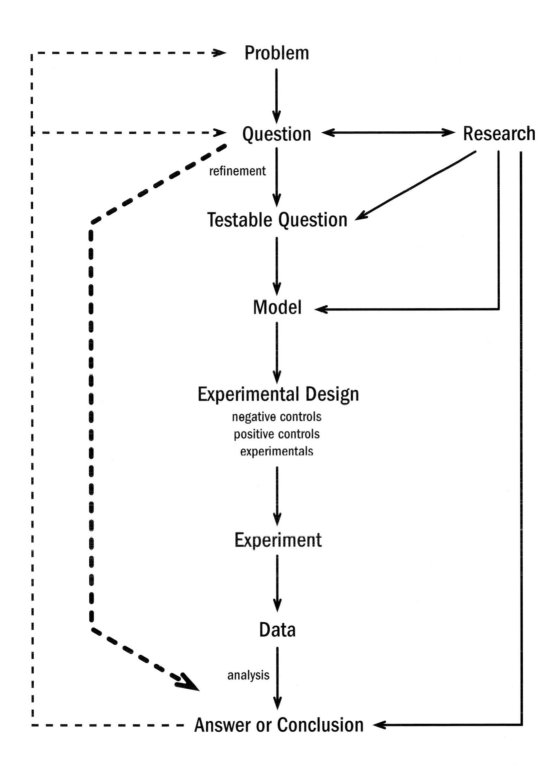

Figure 1.1. The Problem-Solving Flow Chart.

The brains-on approach.

The brains-on method is diagrammed in Figure 1.1. Some people call this the scientific method. The ideas presented in the flow chart are simple. Everybody has problems. We all ask questions. We have done library research or looked up answers to questions. The terminology used in the problem-solving path may be unfamiliar, but we all use problem-solving techniques. Each step is described in detail in later chapters of this book.

Asking a question is the first step in problem solving because the question defines the problem. A question can be analyzed to determine if the answer will be found more readily by experimentation or by researching the findings of others. In some cases the question must be refined, the terms must be defined and clarified before it becomes a testable question. A testable question suggests a hypothesis or model. A hypothesis can be tested by experimentation. If the experiment is properly controlled, it will yield data that should, upon analysis, answer the question. Some questions can be answered directly (see heavy dashed line). Sometimes the answer will lead to further questions or problems (light dashed line). This book will provide a point-by-point description of how to implement the brains-on method starting with questions asked by elementary school students.

Problem solving is not as daunting as it seems.

People solve problems using this method every day. The process is natural to humans. We may not think about solving problems in a formal, diagrammatic manner. We just do it. Children use problem-solving techniques at an early age. For example, one child covets a toy another child is using. The two children can try a number of strategies to get and keep the toy, and probably only some of these techniques will be acceptable to their parents. The problem is getting and keeping the toy. The first question is "How can I get the toy?" A more refined question might be "Can I get the toy by grabbing it?" or "Can I get the toy by asking for it?" The child will brainstorm a number of methods for obtaining the toy. The attempt to commandeer the toy is the experiment. The data or results are whether or not the attempt is successful. Both children will imagine additional experiments.

Although problem solving is a natural ability of humans, this skill can be refined. People who are good at solving problems tend to achieve success. The best part of developing problem-solving skills is that these techniques can be applied to many situations. When I was in graduate school, my advisor told me that the methods I was using in the laboratory would be out-of-date by the time I had finished writing my thesis. He said learning how to solve problems was most important because I could use that skill for the rest of my life. He told me how one of his former graduate students decided to manage his family's farm after completing his doctorate. While this may not be the usual path for someone trained in the academic sciences, the problem-solving skills this former student learned in graduate school would help him in whatever career he chose.

Because problem solving is inherent to human nature, young children can be encouraged to develop these skills at an early age. In this book, problem-solving skills are applied to scientific questions. I encourage parents and teachers to create an environment for doing science that is interesting and challenging, so children can apply their creative talents to learning about the world around them.

What are the advantages to a problem-solving approach?

Many methods can be effectively used to teach children science. Why should parents and teachers expend the extra effort required to develop a problem-solving approach to education? Students are interested in the project because people are naturally interested in their own ideas. The students invent the science for themselves. They start with their own questions and figure out, with help, how to turn those questions into experiments. The students determine which scientific concepts they are studying. They analyze their data and draw conclusions for themselves. The experiment becomes the students' creation, not something imposed by an external source.

Problem solving is empowering for students because it encourages logical and critical thinking. The process of refining a question that I describe in Chapter 2 requires that students analyze their ideas and use specific language. Students can apply problem-solving techniques to all aspects of education and life. The ability to analyze data and draw one's own conclusions has value far beyond the completion of an elementary school science project. The problem-solving approach encourages creativity because the students have to figure out how to answer their own questions.

The brains-on method described in this book avoids the performance aspect of demonstrating experiments to students. If the experiment does not "work," it is not necessarily the demonstrator's fault. Everyone has worked together to plan and do the experiment; everyone can work together to fix it. In the real scientific world, not every experiment "works," but unsuccessful experiments may have value. Experiments can usually be repeated and improved. Scientific mistakes and failures sometimes lead to important discoveries. Albert Einstein said, "Anyone who has never made a mistake has never tried anything new."

In the following chapters of this book, I provide a step-by-step description of how to implement the brains-on approach. Most of the examples were derived from questions asked by elementary school children. The science questions I collected from elementary school children are listed in Appendix 1. Appendix 2 is a sample laboratory notebook.

NOTES

1. I. Wilmut, A. E. Schnieke, J. McWhir, A. J. Kind, and K. H. S. Campbell, "Viable Offspring Derived from Fetal and Adult Mammalian Cells," *Nature* 385 (1997): 810–13; Alexander Newman, "Double Takes," *National Geographic World* 289 (1999): 12–15.

2. Maxwell Eden, *Kiteworks: Explorations in Kite Building and Flying* (New York: Sterling Publishing Company, Inc., 1989); Jack Challoner, *Make It Work! /Flight* (New York: Scholastic, 1995).

3. John Bonnett Wexo, "Animal Babies," *Zoobooks* 13 (1996): 1–17; John Bonnett Wexo, "Baby Animals 2," *Zoobooks* 11 (1994): 1–17.

4. Joanna Cole, *The Magic School Bus in the Haunted Museum: A Book about Sound* (New York: Scholastic, 1995); Neil Ardley, *The Science Book of Sound* (San Diego: Harcourt Brace Jovanovich, Publishers, 1991); Andrew Haslam, *Make It Work! Sound* (Chicago: World Book, 1997).

2

Questions

*Imagination is the highest
kite one can fly.*

—Lauren Bacall

CHILDREN ASK MANY CHALLENGING QUESTIONS AS THEY ATTEMPT TO UNDER-
stand their large and confusing world. When my sons were toddlers, they
seemed to say "no" to everything. Then, seemingly overnight, they switched
to asking "why?" "Why do horses have big heads?" "Why does the spider jump?"
"Why are they called May apples?" The questions continue. "Are there bald eagles
in California?" "What are atoms made of?" "How do helicopters fly without wings?"
"Do jellyfish have eyes?" "Have you ever wondered why the planets formed?" My
husband and I often had to admit that we did not know the answers. Some of the
questions led to excursions to the bookstore, library, or World Wide Web. Others
have become the basis for home experiments.

In the midst of this barrage of questions, I learned an important lesson. I
learned that the value of asking a question may be greater than getting the answer,
that asking a question is an initial, powerful step in the learning process. By asking
a question, a child has demonstrated an interest in the subject. In order to ask a
question, the child must organize his or her thoughts and figure out just what aspect
of the subject is confusing. In verbalizing a question, the child may explain the concept to himself or herself. How often have we said or heard, "Oh, never mind, I just
figured it out"? Curiosity is often the first stage in comprehension.

I also learned that the response to a question is important. Replying, "I don't know, *but maybe we can find out"* can encourage creativity and reinforce the value of wonder. This answer communicates that the child's ideas and curiosity are significant and interesting. Maintaining this open-minded attitude under rapid-fire assault by children's questions can be difficult, but recognizing the children's interests is essential to keeping them involved in the project.

Much of education is based on encouraging students to answer questions, because by answering questions, students demonstrate what they have learned. The ability to answer questions effectively is indisputably a useful skill. Perhaps an equally useful skill, however, is the ability to formulate and refine questions—to ask the best questions. To ask a good question, students must figure out what they know, what they do not know, and why they do not know it. They have started to organize, analyze, and store the information for themselves. They have started to learn. When we encourage children to develop their natural skills in designing and asking questions, we may go beyond testing and advance learning.

What is the relationship between asking questions and doing science? I do not recall from my own education any formal training to develop my skills in asking questions, and yet to a scientist, asking questions is of critical importance. Questions are the seeds from which new experiments grow. Carefully cultivated questions aid in experimental design and data analysis. These questions clearly define a problem and point toward approaches for solving the problem. In this way, asking questions becomes the first step in problem solving.

The talent for asking good questions is not innate. It can be encouraged, taught, learned, and developed throughout life. Children come ready-made with curiosity, but they may need to be encouraged to improve their question-asking skills.

In this book, I suggest using children's questions as a basis for designing experiments. Many science materials for children are organized in a question-and-answer format with both the question and answer provided. I prefer an approach starting with children's questions, engaging their help to clarify concepts, and working with them to design solutions. This method starts with the children's interests and lets them learn through investigation. The children are involved in every step of the experimental process, from asking the initial question through presenting the final answer. This approach may retain the child's interest as well as develop creative and intellectual problem-solving skills.

What is a good question?

A good question suggests a strategy, either by research or experiment, to solve a problem. A good question is specific, and describes a testable idea. A good question invites an informative answer, not a vague generalization. A good question is a tool to obtain the desired answer. A good question clarifies the problem, and introduces related ideas.

How do we ask questions?

We ask questions when we are faced with a problem, something that does not fit with our personal model of how the world works. Asking a question is like trying to scratch a mental itch. Something is bothering us, and we're trying to fix it. If we don't get the answer we want, the itching doesn't stop, and we may try to ask the question in a different way. The question at first may be quite general, using terms that are not well defined. This question probably will not result in the desired answer. If the question is made more specific, it can be researched or tested with experiments, and we can obtain the missing information. We can scratch the mental itch. Refining the question may require several attempts.

Imagine several children sledding on the first snowy day of winter. The children have brought several different types of sleds, and they are trading them. The problem is figuring out how to have the most fun. Fun is a vague term that has different meanings for different people. Let's define fun in this case as going down the hill the fastest. The question can be rephrased as *How can I go the fastest?*—or better yet—*Which sled will carry me down the hill the fastest?* The question is now specific, and it defines an experiment. The children can measure how long it takes each sled and rider to go down the hill. They can compare the times and determine which sled is the fastest.

Let's suppose instead that fun is defined as excitement. *How can I have the most exciting ride?* Exciting is a non-specific word in this case because it is difficult to measure excitement directly. What is excitement? Speed? Crashes? Spins? The question still needs clarification.

Here is another example. "Is a grasshopper a bug?" This question is clear, but entomologists differentiate between bugs and insects, so let's be specific. An insect is defined by *Funk and Wagnalls Standard College Dictionary*[1] as "Any of a large cosmopolitan class (Insecta) of small to minute air-breathing arthropods . . . having six

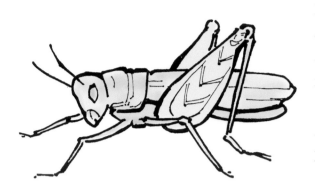

legs, a body divided into a head, thorax, and abdomen, and one or two pairs of wings or none." Bugs are defined as "terrestrial or aquatic insects with piercing, sucking mouth parts." A grasshopper is an insect because it has six legs and a body that is segmented into three parts. A grasshopper does not have "piercing, sucking mouth parts." An experiment appropriate for very young children would be to examine pictures of grasshoppers (or better yet, real grasshoppers in magnifying boxes) and count the legs and body segments. If their data are six legs, three body segments, and no piercing, sucking mouth parts, then their conclusion is that grasshoppers are insects.[2] This experiment is manageable by any child who can count to six.

Not all questions lead to experiments.

A simple answer may suffice for some questions, although it is surprisingly difficult to find children's questions that fall in this category. Many seemingly simple ques-

tions can be turned into research projects or experiments. The most important consideration is what answer will satisfy the questioner.

"Where do sharks poop?" Some clarification of terms may be necessary. Sharks excrete their wastes into the ocean. This subject probably requires no further research.

"What is the most valuable gem?" Valuable can be defined as being worth the most money, or being the most useful for industrial purposes. In either case, the diamond would probably be the answer. If the question is interpreted as which specific stone is the most valuable, research is required. As we cannot auction off the Hope Diamond or the crown jewels to determine this for ourselves, we have to accept published estimates for the worth of these gems.[3]

For many questions, research is the preferred approach. "Why did *Homo habilis* go naked outside?" This question does not require much refinement. *Homo habilis*, or skillful man, lived in Africa about two million years ago. *Homo habilis* are extinct so we cannot experiment on them directly, ethics aside. The only information we have of these early hominids is from the fossil record. There is no evidence that they had invented clothing, but of course we cannot know for certain. Paleontologists believe that the climate was mild in the areas where *Homo habilis* lived, and protection from the elements may not have been necessary.[4]

Library research is also best suited for "What are a rhino's horns made of?" Rhinoceros are not only an endangered species, but they and their horns are not readily available for experimentation. The importation of endangered species or parts of their bodies is illegal. It is known, however, that the rhino's horn is made of thousands of tightly packed strands of keratin. Keratin is a tough, indigestible protein. Fingernails, toenails, and hair are also made of keratin. The  rhino's horn is solid keratin, and does not have a soft, spongy core like the horns of other animals.[5]

Some questions are too difficult to be answered with a simple hypothesis and experiment. Difficult questions can be approached by asking: "What *can* we learn?" and "Is part of the question more manageable?" Some research may be required. For example, "How do you cure AIDS?" is a question many people would like to answer. The disease caused by Human Immunodeficiency Virus (HIV-1) is complex, affecting many of the body's functions and defenses (Figure 2.1). While there is no cure for AIDS at the time of this writing, scientists have developed several effective treatments. How did they do it? Their strategy was similar to that used by the Rebel Alliance in *Star Wars* to defeat the Death Star in Episode 4. The Rebel Alliance stole the plans for the Death Star, analyzed them for weaknesses, and attacked the most vulnerable part. Similarly, scientists started by studying the virus, and analyzing the molecular blueprint within its genetic code. They devised a model of how the virus functions in infection, identifying critical characteristics and potential vulnerabilities. Drugs such as AZT and protease inhibitors are designed to inhibit specific functions of HIV-1. Perhaps these drugs are the molecular equivalents of small, mobile X-wing starfighters that flew up a channel in the middle of the Death Star and fired torpedoes at its thermal exhaust port.[6] While it is unlikely that primary school children will be curing fatal diseases or designing futuristic space weapons, their questions can be refined to become the basis for a strategic attack on a problem. May the force be with them!

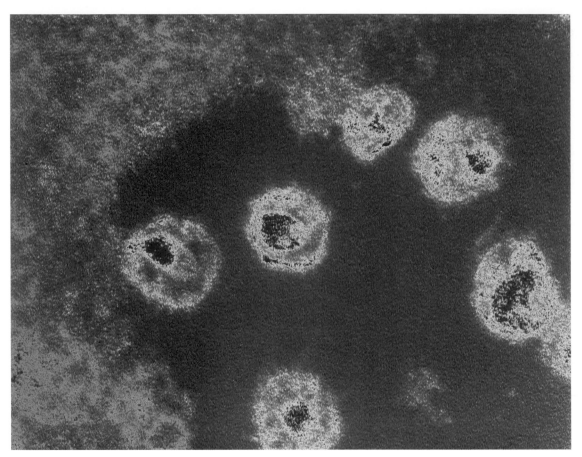

Figure 2.1. Human Immunodeficiency Viral Particles (the AIDS virus). This electron micrograph is the generous gift of Dr. Robert F. Garry.

"Why are leaves green?" is a complex question that can be examined in at least two ways. Leaves are green because they contain a chemical called chlorophyll that absorbs red light and transmits green light. One path towards the answer could be to study light, its diffraction by prisms, and why we see things as being different colors. Another direction would be to study chlorophyll, photosynthesis, and how plants turn sunlight, water, and carbon dioxide into sugars, starches, and oxygen.

How to Start

❶ *Choose a subject, or vote on one.*
In a classroom setting, the curriculum may have been decided in advance. The year's science activities may be devoted to plants, butterflies, indigenous animals, etc. The students can devise their own experiments, but they must focus on the chosen

subject. For experiments done by a family or other small group, the best results will be obtained by focusing on specific interests of the children: soccer, sledding, the solar system, etc.

❷ *Provide some background information or help the students research the subject.*
More research may be necessary later, but this is a good time to start. For example, what animals are indigenous to the area? What are the planets in the solar system? Reading or listening to a book on the subject may generate questions. Viewing educational videos or investigating the World Wide Web may also be helpful.

❸ *Request questions from all students or children in the family.*
Prepare a flyer that can be sent home with students or posted in a prominent spot in the home. Request children's questions about science (or a specific scientific topic), and provide space for writing the questions. Allow several days for the children to generate questions. Suggest that the children record their questions as they think of them.

When I collected questions for this book, I did not specify a subject or provide background information. I simply asked for questions about science, thinking that children would ask questions about subjects in which they had an interest. Whether or not you follow steps one and two depends on whether you must focus on a specific topic. I obtained many questions from my sons simply by listening to them and writing down their spontaneous questions. *The important thing is getting questions from the children.* If we start with their questions, we have started with their interest. If we involve them in every step of the process, we may retain their interest.

❹ *Choose a question that is suitable for experimentation.*
We can test which sled goes down the hill the fastest, but we cannot design an experiment to determine the color of *Tyrannosaurus rex*. To increase your chances of getting questions that are suitable for experimentation, collect lots of questions. The students may wish to vote on which question(s) will be used for experimentation. Voting helps keep everyone interested, and partially circumvents the problem of having to choose only a few questions from the many responses collected from a large group. Another way to appease rival factions might be to investigate one subject in a few ways. One group of children could design experiments to compare the relative speeds of sleds while another could investigate steering capabilities.

Remember that not every question can serve as the basis for an experiment.

Not all questions can even be answered. Every question that is the result of creative thought, however, is worthwhile and deserves recognition.

❺ *Analyze questions as a group exercise.*

"What did you mean by fun?" "Oh, so fun means going the fastest on a sled?" Try not to give away what you think the meaning is because there may be more than one interpretation. If fun means avoiding the thorn bush at the bottom of the hill, experiments could also be designed to determine what structural features of a sled improve steering. Get input from everyone on redefining terms, and improving the specificity of the question.

One way to keep the entire group involved is to employ the technique of brainstorming. (See Chapter 3.) In brainstorming, suggestions are requested from all members of the group. After all the ideas have been collected, they are analyzed. First let the children's creativity run wild, then sort out their suggestions.

Questions surface spontaneously when people encounter new or puzzling ideas. Initially, the question may be vague and not testable. By using specific language, the question can be refined so that it becomes the basis for research or experimentation. The sledding example began with the problem of how to have the most fun. When fun was equated with speed, the resulting question, "Which sled goes down the hill the fastest?" defined an experiment. The sledding example will be used throughout the next few chapters to demonstrate model building, experimental design, controlled experimentation, and data collection, analysis and presentation.

The questions I collected from primary school children for the preparation of this book are listed in Appendix 1.

N O T E S

1. *Funk and Wagnalls Standard College Dictionary* (New York: Funk and Wagnalls, 1974).

2. John Bonnett Wexo, "Insects," *Zoobooks* 11 (1994): 1–18; John Bonnett Wexo, "Insects 2," *Zoobooks* 11 (1994): 1–14.

3. Susan Mondshein Tejada (ed.), "Diamond of Doom," *National Geographic World* 265 (1997): 27–31.

4. Robert A. Bell, *The Big Golden Book of Cavemen and Other Prehistoric People* (Racine: Western Publishing Co., Inc., 1991).

5. John Bonnett Wexo, "Rhinos," *Zoobooks* 13 (1996): 4–5.

6. J. J. Gardner, *Star Wars* (New York: Scholastic, 1977).

3 Brainstorming and Experimental

Planning: The Yin and Yang of Science

First plan your work,
Then work your plan.
If you do, it's awfully simple.
If you don't, it's simply awful.

—*Anonymous*

EXPERIMENTAL PLANNING REQUIRES CARE AND ATTENTION TO DETAIL. BRAIN-storming is unbridled creativity. Both thought processes are required for a successful experiment, and they complement each other. In this chapter, I describe how to use the technique of brainstorming to plan experiments.

What is brainstorming?

Brainstorming is a creative, fun, and crazy aid for teaching problem-solving skills and critical thinking. Brainstorming works very well with children. Students using this technique share original thoughts, and build on the ideas others have suggested. Brainstorming fosters teamwork and cooperation, while allowing for personal recognition and self-acknowledgement. Brainstorming is an integral part of the brains-on approach to science, and can be used to refine questions, plan experiments, draw conclusions, or any other time when creative thinking is required.

The concept behind brainstorming is simple.

- Request ideas from everyone in the group.
- Write them down.
- Analyze them later.

Start by posing a question or a problem to the group. Request ideas for the answer or solution. Each suggestion should be written down as stated. Writing down the children's ideas confers importance, and eliminates the possibility of forgetting any of the children's comments. In my experience, it can be difficult to write fast enough to record all of the proposals offered by a spirited group of children. To encourage creative thinking, collect all of the ideas before analyzing them. The possible, impossible, practical, and impractical can be sorted out subsequently. First let the children's creativity run wild. There will be time later for more sober realities. Children may be hesitant to offer ideas if they hear other suggestions discounted. Refraining from offering adult commentary can require practice and restraint. When I feel the need to "set them straight," I close my mouth and start writing.

The children will have many ideas, and all ideas, which are suggested seriously, should be considered seriously. Of course, children can get carried away, and some suggestions may be merely silly or disruptive. Differentiating between the ridiculous and the sublime may require discretion and tact, but most parents and teachers have faced this problem before. Sometimes apparently "silly" ideas can prove to be valuable.

Brainstorming can be used to refine the question: "Can orchids tell when you touch them?" Some leading questions are shown in blue. Possible responses are noted in grey.

Let's consider the question: "Can orchids tell when you touch them?" What do you mean by "tell"?

- *Well, do they know?*
- *Plants don't "know" anything. They don't have brains.*
- *They don't have brains, but they can do things. They shrivel up when it gets too hot, and flowers close at night.*

You are saying that plants can change in ways we can see. They can respond to factors in their environment like light or heat.

- *Yes. Plants are alive, and they do things even if they can't think.*
- *Plants can grow, and they can die. Big deal.*

Let's get back to refining the question. "Do orchids change in a way we can see when we touch them?" Touch them with what?

- *Our fingers.*
- *A pencil.*
- *Molten lava.*

Let's consider these suggestions: fingers, pencil, and molten lava. Any comments?

- *Where are you going to get some molten lava?*
- *Does anybody see a volcano nearby?*

We can't test molten lava, but we could test the effect of intense heat on an orchid.

- *Someone could light a match, blow it out, and touch the hot tip to the orchid.*
- *That wouldn't be as hot as lava.*
- *It would be pretty hot though.*

So, getting back to our question. What have we come up with? "Do orchids change in a way we can see if we touch them with our fingers, a pencil, or a hot match tip? This question is now testable.

A real life example of children brainstorming is presented in Chapter 7 in the experiment addressing "Why is Apple Cider Brown?" I had asked the children in a first grade class if they could think of ways of keeping air away from a cut slice of apple. The first suggestion was, "Put the apple in the refrigerator." I wrote it down. The second suggestion was, "Put the apple up by the moon, in outer space." The children laughed. I quieted them, and wrote "outer space." The other suggestions are listed in Table 7.4. They included: spreading glue or caramel on the apple, wrapping the apple in foil or toilet paper, and putting the apple in water, oil, dirt, a plastic bag, or a box. I stopped taking suggestions when the children started repeating themselves. Next, we analyzed the suggestions. I read back to them, "Refrigerator." I said that because there was no refrigerator in the classroom, we could not test this suggestion in class the next day. Another child pointed out that there is cold air in the refrigerator. Next, I read, "Outer space." There was more laughter. Several children said that we did not have a rocket. I looked at the girl who had made that suggestion, and said, "That would work because there is no air in outer space, but that is another suggestion that we cannot test in the classroom." The remaining ideas were discussed and tested. I was certain that some of the ideas would not "work," but I thought the experiment would be more interesting if a wide range of results was observed.

The idea of putting an apple in outer space may seem silly, but I wanted to recognize the creative thought that inspired it. This child knew that there is no oxygen  near the moon, and applied that knowledge to a new problem. Her idea is the concept behind the vacuum packaging of foods. NASA does many experiments testing the effects of zero gravity and no oxygen on earthly substances. Even ideas that cannot be easily tested may deserve recognition.

Another silly idea to my mind was wrapping the apple slice in toilet paper. I was sure it would not keep air away from the apple slice, but I thought we could later talk about porous substances, and perhaps try to blow air through a sheet of toilet paper. I was surprised at how well toilet paper worked to prevent browning. At present, I have no explanation for this phenomenon.

In the best possible case, the analysis of the children's suggestions is done with input from the entire group. Brainstorming should be done with care and consideration. No suggestion should be ridiculed. Even ideas that seem silly may prove to be interesting. Think of how the Wright brothers must have felt when they first proposed the airplane.

Experimental planning: think before you leap, then look, then leap.

It is often tempting to jump right into an experiment, but the results will be far more meaningful if the experiment is first planned carefully. Planning an experiment should involve answering the following questions:

- How do you think it works?
- What has research told us about this system?
- Do you still think it works that way?
- Are there other possibilities for how it works?
- Can the model (or hypothesis) be tested?
- How can the model be tested?
- Will the experimental results differentiate between our model and another?

- Is there a way to disprove the models?
- What are potential problems with the test?
- What are potential problems with the data?

This list may seem technical and difficult, but it can be managed in a fun and creative way if brainstorming is used to encourage students to answer the questions. The teacher or parent can lead the students through the list, and obtain the necessary information in a non-threatening way. The first three questions involve gathering information. The remaining seven questions develop problem-solving skills. Dividing the brainstorming session into more than one period may be helpful. Students who are fatigued will not be effective at brainstorming. On the other hand, it is not useful to disrupt the creative flow of ideas in an enthusiastic class. The decision about whether to continue brainstorming or to move on to other activities should be dictated by the children's behavior. Remember there is often a benefit to "sleeping on" a difficult problem.

Let's consider these questions in reference to the sledding experiment. The remainder of this example has been written as an imagined dialog. Questions from the experimental-planning list are shown in bold type.

How do you think it works? Why does a sled go down a snow-covered hill?
- *Sleds slide down a hill because it's slippery.*
- *There is not much friction on snow and ice. We learned about friction last year.*
- *Gravity pulls the sled down.*

So, sleds slide down a hill because there is little friction on snow and ice, and because gravity pulls them downward. I have some books on friction. I'd like everyone to look at them and come up with at least one fact about friction.

The class's research on friction[1] provided the following information.

- When things rub against each other, there is friction.
- The amount of friction produced is proportional to how hard things rub against one another.
- Smooth things rubbing together produce less friction than rough things rubbing together.

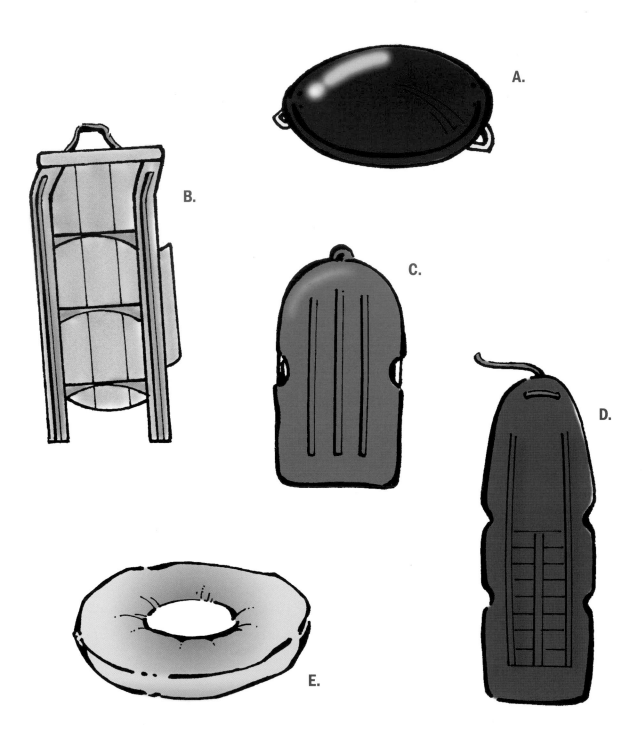

Figure 3.1. The Sleds Used in the Sledding Experiment. A is Saucer Works, B is L. L. Bean, C is Ziffy Whomper, D is SML, and E is Outdoor Outfitter.

- If there is too much friction, the two things cannot move or slide at all.
- Friction produces heat.
- Lubrication reduces friction.

As it turns out, a sled slides down a hill on a thin film of water between the bottom of the sled and the ice. The water acts as a lubricant. The water is produced when the heat of friction melts the ice and snow. On very cold days when it is harder to melt the snow, the sled will not go as fast.[2] Now let's examine the sleds we are going to use. This is what they look like on the bottom (Figure 3.1).

Note the differences in the surfaces that touch the snow. Some have big runners, some have little runners, and some are smooth. The weights of the sleds are listed in the table. I want to thank the students who weighed the sleds, and converted their weights from pounds to kilograms. We all need to become familiar with the metric system.

Table 3.1. The Weights of the Sleds

SLED	WEIGHT (LB)	WEIGHT (KG)
Ziffy Whomper	3.5	1.6
Saucer Works	1.0	0.46
Outdoor Outfitter	2.0	0.91
SLM	3.0	1.4
L. L. Bean	13	5.9

Do you still think it works that way? Are there other possibilities for how it works? Friction or the lack of it seems to play a big part in sledding. Can anyone propose a model or hypothesis about which sled will be the fastest?

- *I think the Saucer Works sled will be the fastest because it has the smoothest bottom.*
- *I think the lightest sled will be the fastest.*
- *I think the red sled will go the fastest.*

I wrote down "smoothest bottom," "lightest," and "red." Let's consider these three models. Our research suggests that model 1 may be correct because less friction is produced when smooth things rub against one another. Model 2 may also be correct because the heavier sleds rub against the snow harder and produce more friction. Would anyone like to comment on the color of the sled?

- *Color doesn't have anything to do with speed.*
- *How do you know?*
- *It just doesn't.*
- *Then why do so many people buy red sports cars?*

We can consider all three models. We'll see if we can prove any of them right or wrong. Let's write the three models on the chalkboard.

- *Model 1: The Saucer Works sled will go the fastest because it has the smoothest bottom.*
- *Model 2: The Saucer Works sled will go the fastest because it is the lightest.*
- *Model 3: The Saucer Works sled will go the fastest because it is red.*

Can the models be tested?

- *Yes. We can compare the speed of the sleds.*

How can the models be tested?

- *We could bring the sleds to a hill on a snowy day and see which one went the fastest.*
- *We could measure the time it took each sled to go down the hill, and compare.*
- *If the Saucer Works sled won, we'd know it is the fastest.*

Should we race the sleds, or should we do them one at a time and compare?

- *Race them!*
- *The last time I raced, my run was longer than the others. It wasn't fair.*
- *Parts of the hill are steeper than other parts.*
- *If we race them, we would need to make all the runs exactly the same, and that would be hard.*
- *Some kids may be stronger pushers or better at steering than other kids.*

You are saying that we want to measure which sled is the fastest, not which run is the best or which child is the best at sledding.

- *We should use the same course for all the runs.*
- *And, the same person should do all the runs.*
- *Can that person be me? Can I ride the sleds?*
- *A race would be fun.*

Will our results tell us which model is correct?

- *No. The Saucer Works sled is all three things. It has the smoothest bottom, it is the lightest, and it is the only red sled.*

If the Saucer Works sled is *not* the fastest, we can assume all of the models are incorrect. If the Saucer Works sled is the fastest, however, we will not be able to tell which model is correct. Is there a way to differentiate between the three models? Can we disprove any of the models?

- *What do you mean?*

Let's say we test the speed of the sleds, and the Saucer Works sled is the fastest. Can we tell *why* it is the fastest? Is it because the bottom is the smoothest, or because it is the lightest, or because it is red?

- *Well, if the Saucer Works sled is the fastest, it is because it has the smoothest bottom.*
- *It is also the lightest.*
- *And, it's the only red sled.*

Are we comparing apples and oranges here?

- *No, we're comparing sleds.*

I mean, there are a lot of differences between the sleds, their shape, their weight, and their color. How do we know what we are comparing? How can we compare just smoothness, or just weight, or just color?

- *We could make the bottom of the Saucer Works sled rougher and see if it is still as fast.*
- *We could make the Saucer Works sled heavier.*
- *We could get a Saucer Works sled in another color, or paint one.*
- *We could make the heavier sleds lighter.*

Exactly! Let's go back and analyze your ideas. How could we make the bottom of the sled rougher?

- *Use sandpaper.*
- *Melt it with a blowtorch.*
- *Glue something rough, like gravel, to the bottom.*

Let's consider these ideas: sandpaper, blowtorch, and gravel. Any suggestions?

- *Sandpaper would make it a little rougher, not much.*
- *Using a blowtorch would be fun!*
- *A blowtorch would ruin the sled.*
- *Gravel would work if we could get it to stick.*

Okay. What about making the sled heavier?

- *You could put rocks on it.*
- *And when you crash, you're going to land on top of the rocks.*

Let's get all the ideas down and analyze them later. Okay?

- *You could put books on it.*
- *You could wear a heavy backpack.*
- *You could change the weight of the backpack so that all the sleds were the same.*

You want to keep the total weight constant. For the light sleds, the rider would wear a heavy pack; and for the heavy sleds, the rider would wear a light pack, so that the total weight is the same. Can anyone comment on rocks, books, and backpacks?

- *What happens if you crash? Who wants to land on rocks?*
- *Or books?*
- *Landing on a backpack wouldn't be too bad.*
- *Go ahead.*

If the weight of the sled determines the speed, which sled should be the slowest?

- *L. L. Bean is a lot heavier than the others.*
- *I bet L. L. Bean is going to be the slowest.*

Does anyone have any ideas about sled color?

- *We could paint the Saucer Works sled a different color, like gold.*
- *I have a blue one at home.*
- *If the blue one is as fast as the red one, then the color doesn't matter.*

What about making the heavy sleds lighter?

- *We couldn't do that without breaking them.*

What have we decided? Changing the smoothness or the shape of the sleds will be difficult. There are a couple possibilities for investigating the weight of the sleds. We could have the rider wear a backpack to make him or her heavier when riding the lighter sleds. Also, if model 2 is correct, then the heaviest sled should be the slowest. We can test model 3 by comparing the speed of our red Saucer Works sled to the speed of a blue one.

What about the *area* of the sled bottom that touches the snow? The L. L. Bean sled rides on wooden runners, but for the other sleds, almost the entire bottom of the sled touches the snow. Do you think that there will be more friction produced when a larger surface touches the snow?

- *Probably.*
- *The area of the sled bottoms is something else we can't really change.*
- *How do we know what the areas are? My brother has homework problems like that, but he's in middle school.*

Let's leave this problem until after we do the experiment. If the L. L. Bean sled is the fastest, we will have to revise our models. If the area of the sled bottom turns out to be an important factor, I'll give you a preview of geometry.

What are some potential problems with the test? Will the sled with the smoothest bottom or the lightest sled, or the red sled be the fastest on wet, or icy, or thin-and-grassy snow?

- *I don't know.*
- *Why does it matter? We're going to test all the sleds on the same day, so we will just use whatever the snow is like on that day.*

What about the condition of the hill? At the beginning of the experiment, the run will be in powder, at the end it will be on packed ice? Do sleds go faster in powder or on ice?

- *On ice.*
- *The sleds tested last will have the fastest times.*
- *We could make a sled run before we start. We could go down the hill a few times to pack the run.*
- *We could test all the sleds twice, and do them in the same order, so that the first sleds would get a chance on the icy run.*
- *Let's test them all three times.*

So, we are going to make a sled run before we start. We will test each sled on the run, then repeat the test two more times. The sleds will be tested in the same order each time.

What are some potential problems with the data? We talked earlier about wanting to measure the differences between the sleds, not the differences between runs or riders. What can we do to make the sled runs consistent? How can we make the sled runs differ as little as possible from each other?

- *The same person should do all the runs.*
- *Can I do the runs?*
- *Someone should time the runs.*
- *We should use a stopwatch.*

- *I want to be the timer.*
- *All the runs need to be the same length, so we need to start and stop them at the same place.*
- *We should mark the start and finish lines with sticks.*
- *Then the person with the stopwatch will know when to start and stop the clock.*
- *We need a person at the top to say, "Go!" so the person riding the sled and the person timing the runs will start at the same time.*
- *The person riding the sled should push off the same way for each run.*
- *And the rider should use the same number of pushes each time.*
- *I always push off three times.*

So, we will choose a person to do all the runs. That person will try to push off exactly the same way for all the runs. We will decide on a number of pushes, maybe three, so the rider can be as consistent as possible. The start and finish lines will be marked, and a person using a stopwatch will time each run as carefully as possible.

If the Saucer Works sled is the fastest, it will be difficult to attribute the cause solely to one of the models. In order to confirm model 1, the structure of an identical saucer sled would have to be altered so that the bottom was rougher. The smooth and rough sleds could then be directly compared. To prove or disprove model 2, the weights of the sleds must be normalized by adding ballast to the lighter sleds. If model 2 is correct, then all sleds that weigh the same should have about the same speed, regardless of their shape. Model 2 predicts that the heaviest sled will be the slowest. Model 3 can be discounted by testing saucer sleds of different colors.

Not every question can be answered with a single experiment. The important thing is to analyze the problem carefully. The problem-solving skills developed in this type of exercise are as vital as knowing absolutely why one sled is the fastest. Sometimes more than one model may factor into the result. The saucer sled may be the fastest because the bottom is the smoothest, *and* because it is the lightest.

Anticipating potential problems with the models, the experiment, or the data is often helpful. Sometimes the design of the experiment can be changed to circumvent pitfalls before they occur. Some problems cannot be predicted in advance. For example, one sled was so difficult to steer that it often could not be kept on the course.

Focus on what the experiment is testing, and to make all other things as similar as possible. The question is "Which sled goes down the hill the fastest?" not "Which child is the best at riding a sled or choosing a run?" In subsequent chapters, the sledding experiment is used to illustrate experimental controls, data analysis and presentation.

NOTES

1. Tillie S. Pine and Joseph Levine, *Friction All Around Us* (New York: Whittlesey-House, 1960).

2. Frank Philip Bowden and David Tabor, *Friction: an Introduction to Tribology* (Garden City: Anchor Press/Doubleday, 1973).

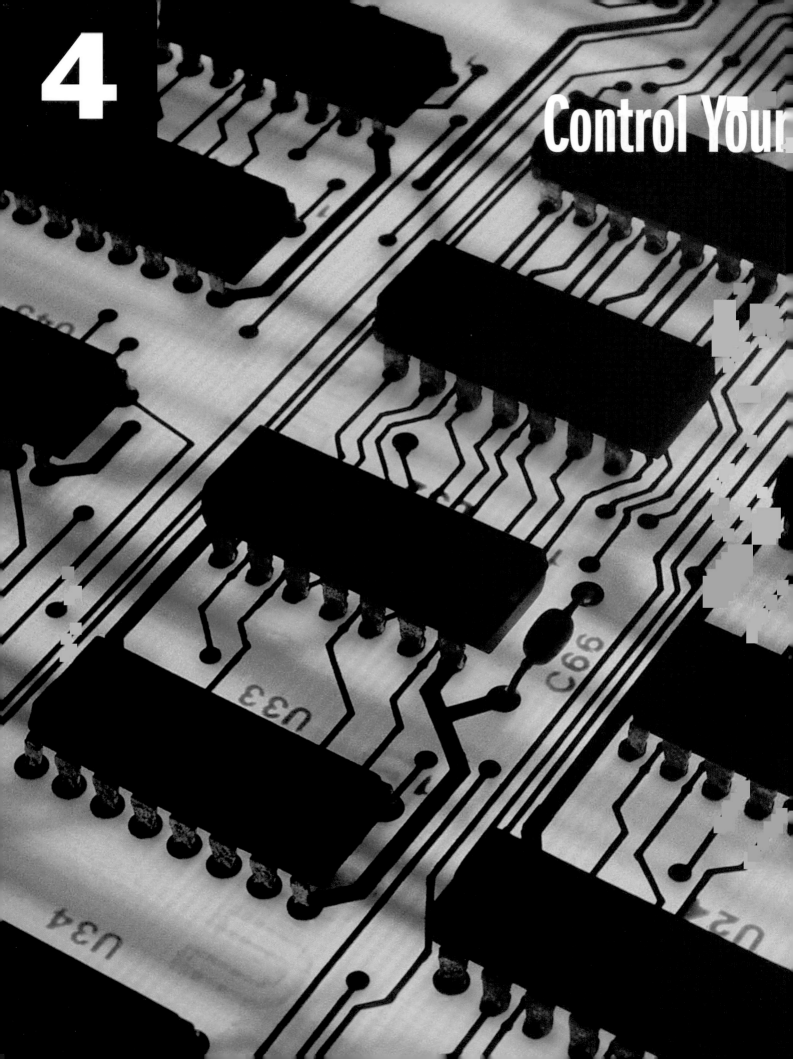

Experiment

STONE TELLING

How do we tell if a window is open?

Just throw a stone at it.

Does it make a noise?

It doesn't?

Well, it was open.

Now let's try another . . .

CRASH!

It wasn't!

—*Shel Silverstein*[1]

Controls are essential.

Experiments are designed to answer a specific question, so it is important to determine whether the answer to the question is correct. Experimental controls confirm scientific results, and convert an experiment into a self-contained argument for a conclusion. Much of the logic and power of the scientific method are embodied in the use of experimental controls.

What are experimental controls and why are they necessary? Controls are additional samples or trials included in the experiment to verify the results. They are the checks and balances that ensure that the data are meaningful. Experimental controls test the scientist's assumptions, and provide the most logical comparison for the test samples. Non-scientists may think of these samples as "extra work." To scientists, controls are a crucial part of the experiment because controls provide the only means to determine if the answer is correct. Control your experiment. Don't let incorrect assumptions control your thinking.

- Controls ensure that the experiment measures what it is intended to measure.
- Controls test whether the experiment is working.

- Controls provide appropriate comparisons for the experimental samples.
- Controls demonstrate whether or not the answer is correct.

Consider the poem by Shel Silverstein. In order to use this method to test whether a window is open, both results must be detected. The absence of sound may imply an open window, but to know for certain, there must be something to compare to the silence. Another noise could mask the sound of breaking glass, or the observer might be too far away from the window to hear the crash. A properly designed experiment would include at least three windows: one window that the stone thrower knows is open, one window that the stone thrower knows is closed, and one window that the stone thrower is testing. Once the stone thrower knows what sounds to expect from the open and closed windows, he can test an "unknown" window with confidence that the results will be meaningful.[2]

Negative and positive controls

There are two types of controls, negative controls and positive controls. Negative and positive controls test different aspects of experimental design.

- *Negative controls measure the background signal in an experiment.* Is there no sound when the rock is thrown at an open window? Are there other street noises that could be mistaken for the sound of breaking glass?
- *Positive controls test whether the experiment is working.* Can the sound of breaking glass be heard when the rock is thrown at a closed window? How loud is the sound? Is the sound of breaking glass easy to identify? Did the window break?

Negative and positive controls mark the expected boundaries on the data. The negative control is done under conditions that should not cause the effect. This is usually the bottom boundary on the data. The positive control results in a measurable effect. This is often the top boundary on the data. The experimental or test samples will probably fall between the two boundaries.

Negative controls are essential components of every experiment.

Negative controls measure background. In other words, negative controls test whether the result was caused by the experimental treatment. Negative controls ensure that the scientific observation was not a random occurrence unrelated to the experiment. People naturally assume that actions have consequences. Negative controls test the assumption that the data are a direct consequence of the experimental treatment. Scientists determine the background signal for an experiment by designing experimental trials that are specifically intended to fail. In most cases, failure is achieved by omitting a critical component from the experiment. Negative controls are used because experimental signals that are not above background are probably not meaningful.

Pretend a new math curriculum has been designed to help children learn multiplication. A group of third grade children are tested on multiplication at the beginning of the school year. The new math curriculum is used during the school year, and the children are tested again at the end of the year. The negative control is the test given at the beginning of the school year. The results of this test indicate the background, or how skilled the children were at multiplication before being exposed to the new teaching method. The critical component that was omitted from this negative control is the implementation of the new curriculum. The test was designed to examine sophisticated multiplication skills, and the students were not intended to be able to pass at the beginning of the year. This negative control tests the assumption that the new curriculum is effective. If most of the students were able to "ace" the test in the fall, then the scores obtained in the spring provide no useful information about the utility of the new math program.

Experiments frequently require more than one negative control, so include as many controls as the children can design. Each essential component of an experiment can be individually omitted. The invention of negative controls is an exercise in logic requiring that children consider the function of every component in their experimental system.[3]

What are positive controls, and why are they useful?

Positive controls test the experimental system, and determine whether or not it will work. Think of positive controls as quality control for the experimental method.

Positive controls are samples that are intended to work very well. What if they do not work? Failure of positive controls is usually caused by improperly designed experiments. Positive controls are useful because they explain why experimental samples fail. In some cases, experiments fail not because the idea behind them was incorrect but because of a technical flaw. Positive controls help fix experiments. The use of positive controls implies a willingness to re-do and improve an unsuccessful experiment until it provides an adequate answer to the question.

Carefully constructed positive controls help point out where the mistake was made. Let's return to the math tests. A positive control would be the inclusion of a few math problems that require no prior knowledge of multiplication. This control monitors testing conditions. Was the reading level of the students adequate to comprehend the questions? Were their pencils sharp enough to write the answers? Were the students alert, focused, and trying to do well on the test? If the students cannot solve addition and subtraction problems, then their failure to solve more difficult problems cannot easily be interpreted. When the positive control fails, the experiment (or math test) may have to be repeated under improved conditions.

Additional trials designated as positive controls are not absolutely essential for every experiment. Test samples may serve as positive controls, as long the experiment is working well enough to produce data. Including positive controls becomes important when the experiment does not work. Designing positive controls for as many aspects of the experiment as possible allows scientists to troubleshoot problems more effectively. For example, if the students can write their names at the top of their math tests, then their pencil points are probably okay. If they cannot solve the non-multiplication questions, then perhaps their ability to read or to concentrate is the problem.

Adding controls to familiar experiments

Consider three experiments frequently done by elementary school children: (1) vinegar and baking soda, (2) batteries and light bulbs, and (3) sprouting beans. Unfortunately, these experiments are rarely done with controls. What are the controls for these experiments?

An experiment has been designed to determine whether orange juice, milk, and apple juice are acidic. When baking soda (sodium bicarbonate) is mixed with acidic liquids like vinegar (acetic acid), a gas (carbon dioxide) is produced, and the mixture foams vigorously. If the chemical reaction is performed in a bottle, the resultant gas can be used to blow up a balloon that has been stretched over the neck of the bottle. Experimenters in a second grade class will determine if gas is produced when baking soda is mixed with orange juice, milk, or apple juice. The negative controls for this experiment are mixing water with baking soda, or vinegar with water. Very little or no gas should be produced in these reactions. The positive control is mixing vinegar and baking soda. The mixture foams, and the balloon inflates as expected. Experimental samples are mixing orange juice, milk, or apple juice with baking soda. The amount of gas produced by the reaction of these liquids with baking soda should be within the range set by the positive and negative controls.

Why is this necessary? If the bottle used for the reactions had been contaminated with some acidic substance (like vinegar from a previous reaction, or cola from the original contents of the bottle), a foaming reaction would occur in every trial. If the negative control (water + baking soda) had been omitted, an incorrect conclusion would be reached, as the experimenters would deduce that all of the test liquids are acidic. What if cornstarch was inadvertently substituted for the baking soda? The two powders look, smell, and feel similar, but when cornstarch is mixed with acidic liquids, no gas is produced. If the positive control (vinegar + baking soda) had not been included, the experimenters would have decided that orange juice is not acidic. Wrong again.

The experimenters tested their assumptions and their experimental system. They verified that the foaming reaction requires two things: an acidic liquid and baking soda. The students assured themselves that the expected result was observed only when both essential components were present. The experimenters can therefore conclude that orange juice is acidic, and that milk and apple juice are not.

A classroom experiment has been designed to determine how many type-C batteries are required to light a 25-watt bulb. What are the appropriate controls for this experiment? A positive control is lighting a small flashlight bulb with a type-C battery. As only one battery is required to light this tiny bulb, this positive control tests whether each battery is in good condition, and if the wire connections have been made correctly. Bulbs can also be pre-tested in lamps

or flashlights to ensure that they are functional. The negative controls are omitting the bulb, batteries, or wires, or not touching the wires to the electrical contacts on the battery and bulb. The negative controls may seem trivial because of our familiarity with electric lights, but the four negative controls allow the students to confirm the requirement for each component of their experimental system. They determine

that batteries, wires, bulbs, and electrical contacts are necessary and sufficient to light a bulb. In subsequent experiments, they can investigate how many batteries are required to illuminate the larger 25-watt bulb.

A first grade class wants to know if bean plants grow faster when planted in sand, forest loam, or commercial potting soil. What controls should they use in this experiment? One negative control is to omit the soil, and germinate some seeds on damp paper towels. Plants produce their own energy through photosynthesis, so beans can grow in the absence of soil. The lack of minerals and the structural stability that soil normally provides will eventually become evident.[4] Another negative control is to omit the beans. Forest loam will contain weed seeds that may resemble bean plants when they are first sprouting. The positive control is the commercial potting soil because it should produce healthy plant growth if the bean seeds are in good condition, and if the amounts of water and light are sufficient. The experimental samples are the beans planted in forest loam or sand. The growth of the bean seeds in these test soils is expected to fall within the range established by the positive and negative controls. (The results of this experiment are presented in Chapter 6 and Appendix 2.)

Using positive and negative controls in children's experiments.

The use of experimental controls is frequently overlooked in children's science, but this omission undercuts the logical framework of the experiment. Children are capable of comprehending experimental controls. Children understand logic and rules, and they naturally make comparisons. The experiment will make more sense if the controls are included because controls provide the appropriate comparisons for the experimental samples. Designing an experiment with controls simplifies data analysis, teaches logic, and strengthens the argument for the conclusion.

Five examples of controlled experiments are described in the remainder of this chapter. In each case, the negative control is used to test the assumption that the observed result was caused by the experimental treatment. The positive controls ensure that the experiment is working.

The apple browning experiment described in Chapters 3 and 7 demonstrates the need for controls. In this experiment, children were asked to think of ways to prevent apple slices from turning brown. The positive control for each test is a freshly cut apple slice. These pale yellow apple slices demonstrate the original color of the apple. They represent the top boundary on the data, or no browning at all. The negative control for each test is an apple slice that had been cut at the same time as the treated slice, but not treated. These darkened apple slices represent the bottom boundary on the data, or maximum browning. When collecting their data, the students compared the color of each treated slice to its untreated and freshly cut counterparts. The controls gave the children standards by which to judge the experimental samples.

In the absence of controls, the data would have consisted of a bunch of cream, tan, or brown apple slices with little basis for comparison. Simply comparing the experimental (treated) apple slices to each other causes two problems. First, the browning reaction is time dependent, so the treatments that were done earliest may be the darkest. Secondly, the experiment would not have conclusively demonstrated whether any of the treatments could prevent browning altogether, or if any of the treatments had no effect on browning. The controls provided a framework for analyzing the data.

What are the negative and positive controls for the sledding experiment? One negative control is sliding down the hill without a sled. In the sledding conditions used for this experiment, a child in snowpants moved only a few inches down the hill, demonstrating that a sled was required to complete the run. Another negative control is omitting the rider. As the hill was rather flat at the top, and the sled could not push off by itself, the riderless sled did not go down the hill at all. A third negative control is measuring the speed of a sled and rider on the first run down the hill, before the track was made. In unpacked snow, the sled and rider could not reach the bottom of the hill without additional pushes. Each negative control omits one essential component of the experiment: the sled, the rider, or the track.

The positive control for the sledding experiment could be an Olympic-style toboggan, or it could be the experimental sleds. Previous experience has shown that all of the sleds will complete the measured run at some speed. If the snow was so thin and patchy that the sleds could not reach the bottom of the hill, then the experiment would simply have to be repeated when the snow was deeper.

The following "plastic box experiment," complete with its controls, was designed and performed by my seven-year-old son. We have a collection of about 150 brick-sized, interlocking plastic blocks. Unfortunately, the blocks also function as boxes, as they have lids that can be opened and snapped shut. Sometimes small toys are placed in the boxes and lost for long periods of time. One day, we speculated that a missing Beanie Baby had been put inside one of the boxes. The problem was how to determine if one of the boxes contained the missing Beanie Baby without opening all of them. The question became, "Can we tell if a Beanie Baby is inside a box by shaking the box?" My son first shook an empty box. This was the negative control. Next, he put another Beanie Baby in a box, closed the lid, shook it, and experienced the sound and feel of a non-empty box. This was the positive control. The remaining boxes were the experimental samples. Unfortunately the experiment was not successful, as we did not locate the missing Beanie Baby. (It was found several weeks later in a binocular case.)

Removing tarnish (oxidized copper) from pennies with lemon juice (citric acid) is frequently suggested as a science project for children. An experiment was designed to determine how long the pennies must remain in lemon juice before they are shiny. Let's consider some potential problems with the experiment, and how the use of controls can circumvent these difficulties. Pennies do get brighter when they are immersed in lemon juice. Will the experimenters be able to tell how much brighter? The cleaning process will not change the appearance of a new penny very much. An old penny will get significantly brighter, but will the experimenters remember how dark it was to start with? The experiment can be done so that the positive and negative controls are displayed on the same coin. If a drop of lemon juice is placed in the center of a tarnished penny, left for several minutes, and washed off, the effect of the acid treatment is

clearly visible. The negative control (the outside ring that was not treated) can be directly compared to the positive control (the spot under the drop of lemon juice). The amount of tarnish removal is obvious. Drops of lemon juice can be left on pennies for increasing periods of time to determine how much time is required to remove the tarnish.

Children seem to love product-testing experiments, perhaps because they are familiar with the format from television commercials. One cautionary note: this type of experiment often becomes an economic analysis. The children determine which product is the best value, and the scientific phenomenon behind the process may be ignored. In the following example, the effectiveness of two brands of laundry detergent is compared. The next experiment investigates how laundry detergent works to remove stains from clothing.

A science teacher has a laundry detergent that works well (brand A), and she receives in the mail a free sample of another detergent (brand B). Brand B is less expensive, and the science teacher wants to know if brand B cleans clothing as well as brand A. To do this experiment, the science teacher needs the two detergents, a washing machine, four new white socks, two small children, and a mud puddle. Perhaps you have guessed the roles of the small children, the socks, and the mud puddle. Before continuing with the experiment, the science teacher confirms that all the socks are equally dirty.

The science teacher washes one sock in brand A. This is the positive control because she knows that brand A gets clothes clean. For the experimental sample, the science teacher washes another sock in brand B. She is testing whether brand B gets the sock as clean or cleaner than brand A. For a negative control, the science teacher does not wash one sock. This control will provide a permanent record of just how dirty those socks were. As the science teacher has one sock left, she decides to do another negative control. This sock is washed with no detergent. This control shows how clean socks get by just sloshing them around in the washing machine. This sock may become as clean as the ones washed with brands A and B. As the experiment is a cost-benefit analysis, this is potentially important information.

Variables such as water temperature, the amount of detergent, and washing conditions should be the same for all trials. To get a definitive answer about which detergent is the best, several socks should be tested in each group. An additional positive control would be to compare the washed socks to new, unused socks. This control tests if any of the treatments get the socks completely clean.

How does laundry detergent remove stains from clothing? Commercial laundry detergents really do contain "bleach, borax, and brighteners," "enzymes," "bleach alternatives," and other chemicals that aid in cleaning clothing. For the purpose of this experiment, we will consider only the function of the detergent.

Liquids can be divided into two classes: watery and oily. A mixture of oil and water will separate, no matter how much the mixture is shaken, and the oil will always rise to the top. This separation is frequently observed when making vinaigrette salad dressings because vinegar is a "watery" liquid that does not mix with salad oil. Many of the chemicals that commonly cause stains are "oily" compounds. Chlorophyll (grass stains), hemoglobin (blood stains), and lycopene (tomato juice) do not dissolve readily in water, so plain water will not remove these chemicals from clothing.

Detergents are a special class of compound, because they have characteristics of both watery and oily liquids. One end of the detergent molecule is watery, while the other end is oily. When detergents are dissolved in water, the detergent molecules arrange themselves into spheres with the watery parts facing outward and the oily parts clustered in the center. Thus, detergents dissolve in water, but maintain an "oily" core in which oily stains can dissolve. The oily stains trapped in the detergent core can be washed away with water. (See Figure 4.1.)

How do detergents remove stains from clothing? Research led to the following model: Detergents remove stains by increasing the solubility of the oily stain in water. The question can be refined to read: "Can we increase the solubility of stain-causing materials in water by adding detergent?" An experiment can now be planned to answer this question.

Cut four equal-sized rectangles out of white coffee filters. Label the filters "no treatment," "water," "water + detergent," and "oil" with ball point pen along one edge. About ½ inch from the opposite edge of each filter, spot a small amount of (1) spinach juice from a package of frozen spinach, (2) tomato juice, (3) blood from a meat package, (4) black ink from a washable felt-tipped marker, and (5) black ink from a "permanent" marker. (See Figure 4.2.) Pour a small amount of water into two flat-bottomed bowls, and cooking oil into a third. Add a few drops of detergent to one of the water bowls and mix. Stand up three of the coffee filters in the appropriate bowls, balancing them against the sides of the bowls. Make sure the spots are not underwater or "under-oil." The "no treatment" filter remains dry. As the liquids are drawn to the top of the paper, they pass through the spots. If the spot is soluble in the liquid, the spot will move up the filter with the liquid. Water with or without detergent will rise to the top of the filter in a few minutes, but it may require several hours for the oil to be drawn to the top of its filter.

One negative control is the "no treatment" filter. In the absence of liquid, none of the spots will migrate, so this filter demonstrates the original position, color, intensity,

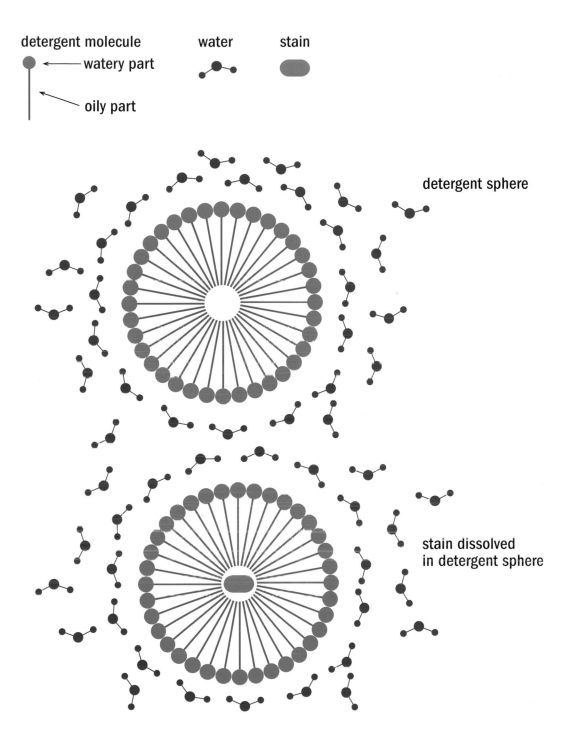

detergent molecule — watery part
oily part

water

stain

detergent sphere

stain dissolved
in detergent sphere

Figure 4.1. How Detergents Work. Detergents remove stains by making the stain-causing substance more soluble in water. Each detergent molecule has two ends: a watery end and an oily end. Dissolving the detergent in water causes the detergent molecules to arrange themselves in a sphere with the watery parts facing outward. The oily stain dissolves in the oily center of the sphere, and is washed away by water.

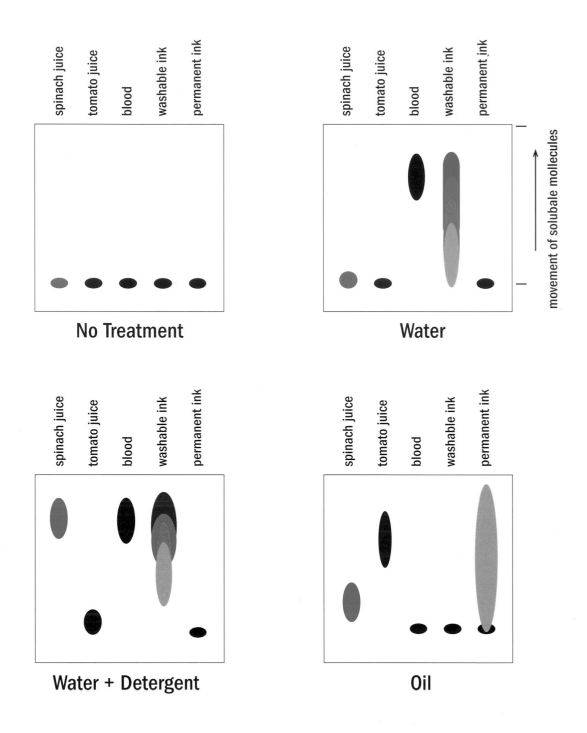

Figure 4.2. The Stain Solubility Experiment. Washable ink is soluble in water and water + detergent. Permanent ink is soluble only in oil. Blood is soluble in water and water + detergent. Grass stains are soluble in water + detergent. Tomato juice is slightly soluble in water + detergent, and very soluble in oil.

and size of the spots. A second negative control is the "permanent" marker on the "water" filter. Permanent ink is not soluble in water, so this ink spot will not change as water is drawn up the filter. The samples spotted on the "water" filter are negative controls for the samples spotted on the "water + detergent" filter. Any differences in the final appearance of the two filters must be attributed to the presence of detergent. A positive control is the spot made by the "washable" marker on the "water" filter. As the water is drawn up the filter, the water-soluble black ink will separate into its component colors.

What happened to the experimental samples? The spinach juice spot did not migrate with plain water, but did move up the filter when detergent was added to the water, demonstrating that chlorophyll is quite soluble in detergent. This sample shows how the oily chlorophyll found in grass stains can be removed from clothing with detergents, but not with plain water. The spinach spot was slightly soluble in oil. The tomato juice spot was insoluble in water, slightly soluble in water + detergent, and very soluble in oil. Removing tomato juice stains from clothing with soap and water is not always successful. The blood spot was drawn up the filter with both water and water + detergent. It did not migrate in oil demonstrating that hemoglobin is less of an "oily" stain than I had thought. The water-soluble marker separated into its component colors in both water and detergent + water, but the color pattern changed when detergent was added. The water-soluble marker was not soluble in oil. The permanent marker was soluble only in oil, although the black ink did not separate into component colors.

Many oily stains are not very soluble in water, so it is difficult to remove these substances from clothing with plain water. There are lots of good reasons for not putting cooking oil in a washing machine, so people use detergents instead. The stain dissolves in the oily center of the detergent sphere while the water-soluble exterior of the detergent sphere allows it to be washed away in water. In effect, detergents mobilize oily stains on clothing just as they did on the coffee filters.

Designing your own positive and negative controls.

When designing controlled experiments, remember the definitions of positive and negative controls. Negative controls measure the background signal in an experiment. Include controls that are intended to fail. Failure can often be assured by omitting an essential component from an experimental trial. Negative controls are more important than positive controls in developing a scientific argument because negative controls prove that the result was caused by the experimental treatment. Positive controls test whether the experiment is working. Include a control that is assured to demonstrate the desired effect. Think about what the question is asking, and make sure the controls will verify the conclusion. Consider how the data will be analyzed and include the relevant comparisons in the experimental design.

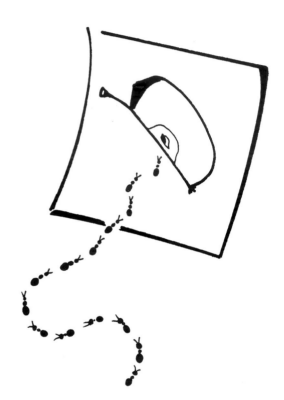

In the following quiz, four science experiments are described.[5] Can you think of negative and positive controls for each experiment? (The answers are listed at the end of the chapter, but please try not to peek until you have thought about the problems.)

Experiment 1: How do ants know where to go when they are following one another?

When an ant finds food, it lays down a pheromone trail from the nest to the food source so that the other ants can locate the food. A small slice of apple is placed on a sheet of paper near an ant trail. "The ants go marching one by one" to the apple slice. The experimenters observe that when the apple slice is moved to a different spot on the paper, the ants go to the original spot before they go to the new location of the apple slice.

Negative control _____

Positive control _____

Experiment 2: How can you tell if common household "chemicals" like toothpaste or cola are acidic or basic?

An acid/base indicator can be prepared by boiling chunks of red cabbage in water, and then filtering the mixture. The resulting purple liquid can be used as an acid/base indicator because the liquid turns pink when mixed with acid, turns green when mixed with base, and remains purple when mixed with neutral substances. A fourth grade class wishes to use their indicator solution to test if toothpaste, cola, aspirin, and tea are acidic or basic. (Hint: this experiment requires more than one positive control.)

Negative control _____

Positive control _____

Experiment 3: How does a compass work?

The magnetic North Pole of the Earth attracts other magnets. If a magnet is free to rotate, like the floating magnetic needle in a compass, it will be attracted to the magnetic North pole, and point north. A needle can be magnetized by stroking it about 30 times on a strong magnet. Hold the needle by the eye, and always stroke it in the same direction across the same end of the magnet. Float a small round piece of paper in a bowl of water, and rest the needle magnet on it. When the needle stops moving, it will be pointing to the north.

Negative control _____

Positive control _____

Experiment 4: When you water a plant, how does the water get from the dirt into the plant?

A popular science demonstration for children illustrates how plants draw water through their stems, and into the leaves. A celery stalk is partially split from the bottom. One side is put in water containing a few drops of blue food coloring, and the other side is put in water containing a few drops of red food coloring. After several hours, half of the celery is blue, and half is red.

Negative control _____

Positive control _____

Controls are what differentiate scientific experiments from magic tricks. Every magic trick has a rational explanation, but the magician hides it, and claims instead that a magic word or the wave of a wand has caused the perceived phenomenon. Have you ever seen a magician do a "no-sleeve" control? Scientists, on the other hand, endeavor to convince themselves and others that the experimental treatment has caused the observed result. Controls make this logical argument possible.

Most scientists learn to use controls through long and sometimes bitter experience, but the rules for their use are not too complex for children. The use of controls is an aspect of science that is appropriate and straightforward to teach to

---

RECIPE FOR EXPERIMENTAL DESIGN

1. A testable experimental question
2. Negative controls (critical component omitted)
3. Positive controls (quality control)
4. Experimental samples

   An experiment is a logical argument for a conclusion bounded by positive and negative controls.

children, but it is neglected in almost all children's science projects. Scientific controls are at the heart of the scientific method.

N O T E S

1.   Shel Silverstein, "Stone Telling," *Where the Sidewalk Ends* (New York: Harper Collins Publishers, 1974).

2.   The author has not tested this particular experiment.

3.   The negative control mentioned in "Stone Telling" is an open window. What critical component was omitted from this trial to ensure its failure? What assumption does this control test?

4.   An additional advantage of the no-soil control is that it allows the children to watch the beans sprout. Observing the formation of small roots and stems enhances the learning experience from this experiment.

5.   Jane Bingham, *The Usborne Book of Science Experiments* (Tulsa: EDC Publishing, 1991). (The experiments used in the quiz [but not their controls] were taken from this book.)

ANSWERS

1. One negative control is a clean sheet of paper. Will the ants ignore a sheet of paper that does not contain food? Will they investigate something that is close to their path? The positive control is the apple slice in its original location. Are the ants hungry? Do they like apples? Will they go where they are "supposed" to go?

2. The negative control is distilled water because distilled water is neither acidic nor basic. (Some tap water is slightly acidic due to impurities in the water.) The positive controls for this experiment are known acidic and basic substances. The acid could be lemon juice or vinegar. The base could be baking soda or ammonia.

3. The negative control is a non-magnetized needle. A non-magnetized needle will not turn to point north. The positive control is a "real" compass. This control will demonstrate which end of the needle is pointing north.

4. The negative control is clear water. If no coloring is put in the water, then the leaves should remain green. Experimental samples can be the positive controls. If the celery leaves do not turn color, then perhaps not enough food coloring was used, or not enough time has elapsed for the water to be drawn through the stem, and into the leaves.

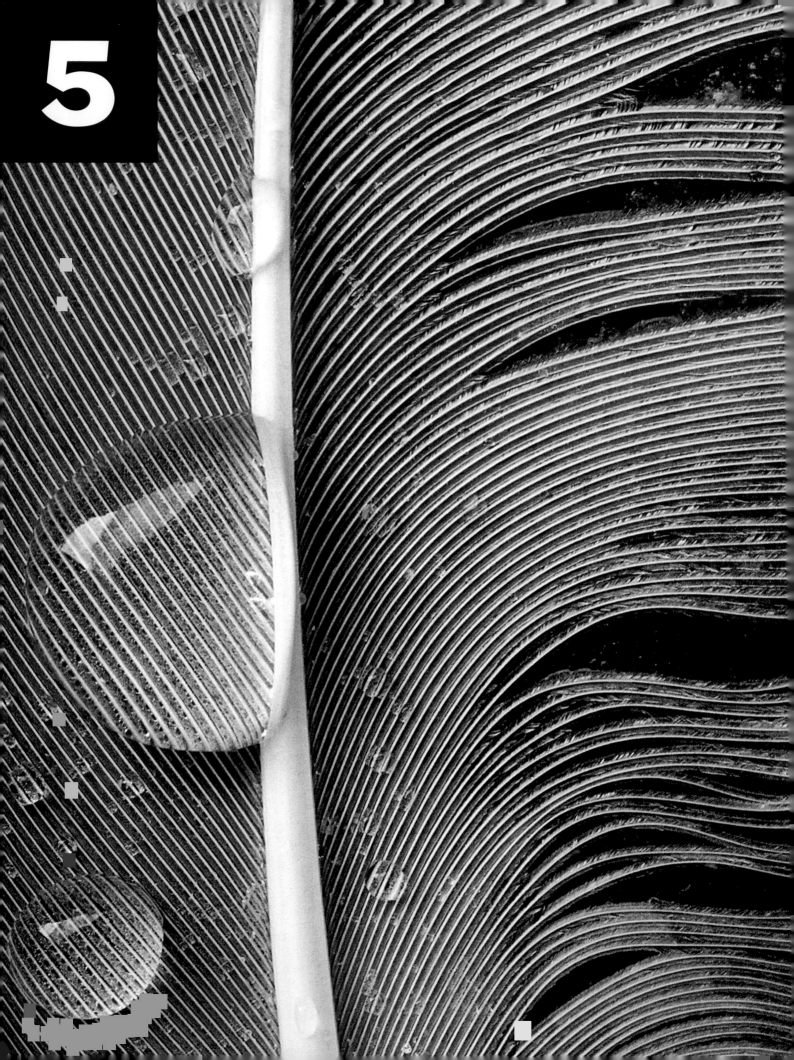

Let's Experiment !

Youth is wholly experimental.

—*Robert Louis Stevenson*

ARE TAKEN IN DEFINING A SCIENTIFIC QUESTION AND PLANNING CONTROLS should result in an experiment that is easy to do and data that are simple to analyze. Doing the experiment involves keeping a laboratory notebook, collecting the data, and coping with experimental error.

Write everything down.

The conventional wisdom about keeping a student laboratory notebook seems to revolve around two main tenets. (1) Each new experiment should begin with the statement "The purpose of this experiment is to demonstrate . . ." (2) Neatness is paramount. I suggest a different tactic. Writing the purpose of the experiment implies that the outcome is known in advance. If experiments are designed to test a hypothesis, then the conclusions will result from a comparison of experimental samples to their controls. Thus, a scientific question is not answered until the experiment is complete. An appropriate title for experiments can be the question that the experiment is designed to answer.

How important is neatness? The student must be able to decipher his notes at a later date. Other people should also be able to read the notebook. Laboratory notebooks, however, are in the thick of things. Reagents are spilled on them, they may

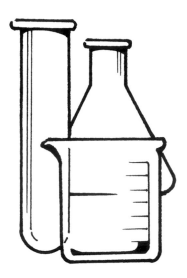

be carried to snow-covered hills, and data are recorded while the experiment is in progress. The final presentation of the data should be neat, orderly, and beautiful, but as long as the notebook is a complete and legible record, its style is unimportant.

A good notebook gives the experimenter control over the experiment, and helps ensure reasonable results. Experimenters should plan their experiments in advance, and write the plans in the notebook. Knowing what you are going to do before you do it often eliminates unwelcome surprises in the laboratory. Valuable skills are developed in devising experimental protocols and learning how to follow them. Similarly, the ability to keep an accurate record of events has applications beyond the completion of an experiment.

Can children keep a laboratory notebook? Students who are learning to write will need help, and older children need direction as well. The maturity level of the students dictates how much assistance they need. Children often like to keep track of information, so recording data comes naturally to them. For young children, compiling a laboratory notebook can be a group exercise, and brainstorming can be used to involve the children.

What should go into a laboratory notebook? Just about everything. Students should be encouraged to write everything down, and never trust their memories. A complete laboratory notebook helps the scientist do the experiment without mistakes, facilitates the analysis of the data, and helps with the presentation of the results. The following list should help students construct and maintain their notebooks.

❶ *The date.* Record the date when the experiment was done.

❷ *A title.* The question the experiment is designed to answer can serve as a title.

❸ *Answers to the list of questions about experimental planning* from Chapter 3. If brainstorming was used to plan the experiment, a condensation of the relevant ideas can go in the laboratory notebook. Most importantly this should include:

- Information obtained from library research. See the list of facts on friction in Chapter 3.
- The model. The student should state how she thinks the system works.
- Considerations about experimental consistency. For the sledding experiment, there should be notations regarding timing the runs, having the same person ride all the sleds, and testing all the sleds three times.

4 *Controls.* List the negative and positive controls that will be included in the experiment. Write down the assumptions that the negative controls are designed to test. What essential components are omitted from the negative controls? Which experimental conditions are supposed to "work"?

5 *Materials and methods.* What is needed to do the experiment? Another scientist wishing to duplicate this experiment should be able to find all of the necessary information in the materials and methods section of the notebook. The list of materials for the sledding experiment would include descriptions and sketches of the sleds, and a notation of any other equipment (stopwatches and calculators) used in the experiment. The methods section should include a detailed report of how the experiment was done. A laboratory notebook for the sledding experiment would include a description of how the sled run was prepared, the name of the rider, the number of pushes the rider used, the length of the hill, how the timing was done, etc.

6 *The data.* Depending on the experiment, the data may be:

- A table of numbers. (In the sledding experiment, the data would be the times required for each sled to complete the run.[1])
- A qualitative analysis. (In the dirty sock and laundry detergent experiment, brand A might be rated + + for cleaning power and brand B rated + + +.)
- A detailed description. (A laboratory notebook for the stain solubility experiment could include a description of the final appearance of the coffee filters, a record of how far the spots moved, and whether the spots changed color as their components separated.)
- Photographs or sketches. (A photograph showing the washed and unwashed socks would clearly demonstrate the results.)

❼ *Notes about the experiment.* Any information that is relevant to the analysis of the data should be included. For example, students doing the sledding experiment should note that one sled could not be kept on course because it was so difficult to steer. Perhaps one laundry detergent turned the socks yellow, or ate holes in them. Any problems that occur while doing the experiment should be recorded in the notebook.

❽ *The analysis of the data.* The laboratory notebook should include sample calculations, tables, and graphs. Data analysis is covered in detail in Chapter 6.

❾ *The conclusions.* Was the question answered? What was learned?

❿ *Notes on future experiments.* Did the experiment lead to more questions? How could they be answered?

Loose-leaf notebooks and notebooks with perforated pages should not be used as laboratory notebooks because pages may be lost. Expensive bound laboratory notebooks with graph paper and carbon copies are not necessary. A simple spiral pad works well as long as extra pages such as graphs, photographs, sketches or computer printouts are taped securely in place.

A laboratory notebook for the bean seedling experiment is provided as an example in Appendix 2.

Be careful. Be consistent.

The experiment should be done as carefully as possible. Small inconsistencies may result in big changes in the data. There is an element of craft in doing experiments and producing beautiful data that can generate as much personal satisfaction as the ability to hit a three point shot or to do the splits. Of course, inexperienced hands may make mistakes especially in the excitement that often accompanies children's experiments. Making a mistake is not the end of the world. Children should be encouraged to take the collection of data seriously, but almost any experiment can be repeated, and perhaps improved in the repetition.

Label all reactions, trials, and controls. Don't trust your memory to distinguish the sock washed in brand A from the one washed in brand B. In the controlled chaos that characterizes children's experiments, samples can be mixed up. When the smoke clears, it will be easier to analyze and double check labeled samples. Do not label the lids of containers, as lids can be removed and separated from the experiment. For samples that are difficult to label, try a creative approach. If several bean seeds are planted in one cup, record the location of each seed with a different colored mark on the rim of the cup. The pennies in the lemon juice experiment can be labeled on masking tape attached to the flip side. "Permanent" markers contain ink that is not soluble in water, so they are often useful in wet experiments.

Safety is always a concern when doing science experiments with children. An adult should handle hazardous chemicals such as strong acids and bases. All persons involved in experiments using potentially dangerous chemicals should wear eye protection, rubber gloves, and lab coats. Experiments that require flames, heat, or electricity should also be monitored closely by an adult. Broken glassware and other sharp objects are potential hazards. In most cases, common sense can ensure that experiments will be safe, educational, and fun.

Well, what about fun? Actually doing the experiment is often the most fun part of the scientific process. It's time to take chances, make mistakes, and get messy. What could be better? Much time and effort has been spent on the experiment since the children first asked the question. Finally learning the answer should be the moment they have all been waiting for.

Leave the anxiety at the door. Because the experiment has been planned and done as a group effort, the stress component should be reduced. The teacher or parent should not feel compelled to demonstrate a perfect experiment. The students should not worry if the data proves their model wrong. The point is to learn something, and learning *is* fun. An elementary school teacher once admitted to me that the chemistry class she had taken in high school had "provided enough stress to last a lifetime." I can remember experiencing a sinking feeling in my own laboratory courses when I realized that I had botched the experiment, and was not going to have enough time or reagents to repeat it. Mistakes happen. Schedule enough time and procure enough supplies so that the experiment can be repeated (and improved) if necessary. Be flexible. It is better to spend a little more time and end up with a successful learning experience, than to hurry on to another subject before the experiment has been done correctly. Creativity is stifled in a tense environment. Real scientists do not produce successful experiments every day. Why should we expect that of children?

Be consistent. Remember what the question is asking, and what the experiment is testing. No other factor should be varied between experimental trials. The sledding experiment was designed to compare the differences between sleds, so conditions were kept as similar as possible from run to run. The same rider made all the runs, the rider pushed off the same way each time, and the length of the run remained the same. The experimenters anticipated that the condition of the snow might change as the experiment progressed, so all the sleds were tested three times, and every sled was tested on packed snow.

The best experiments for children test one thing at a time. The experiment on bean growth is comparing different soils, therefore, all the plants should receive the same amount of water and light, they should be grown at the same temperature, and the pots should all hold the same amount of dirt. The penny brightening experiment is investigating how much time is required to remove tarnish from copper. To ensure consistency, all pennies should be about the same color to start with, and the juice drops should all come from the same lemon. Strive for similarity in all aspects of the experiment except the one that is the subject of the experimental test or control.

Life is imperfect, and so are your data.

Very few experiments work perfectly, although people seem to expect perfection on the first try. Numbers are rarely "spot on," there are glitches, and there are differences between apparently identical trials. Why? There are three main reasons for imperfection. (1) An unknown variable changes between trials. For example, students with little sledding experience may not have anticipated that the hill would get faster with successive runs. (2) Biological variation is also a source of "error." No two living things are exactly alike, even identical twins. Two seemingly identical beans planted in identical conditions may germinate on different days. Biological variation is part of life. These little differences make the world interesting, and allow species to adapt and evolve. (3) Small human errors in making measurements or performing the experiment can affect the data. If the person timing the sled runs did not stop the stopwatch exactly when the sled crossed the finish line, that sled would appear to have a slower time. Glitches are okay; they are inevitable; we need to cope with them.

How do scientists cope with all these errors and differences between samples? They use repeated trials. Repeated trials can aid in understanding variations caused by unknown variables, biological variation, and human error.

An example of a discrepancy caused by an unknown variable can be found in a popular science fair experiment. Children seem to love experiments designed to determine the favorite food of a family pet. (Family pets probably love these experiments too.) An experiment was planned to test whether a guinea pig preferred carrots or cucumber slices. Every morning for a week, the experimenter put the two foods in  opposite corners of the cage, and recorded which vegetable the guinea pig ate first. Let's pretend that one morning the experimenter was unaware that her younger sister had already fed the guinea pig, and on this day the sated rodent was indifferent to the treats. If a single trial had been used, the experimenter might erroneously conclude that the guinea pig liked neither carrots nor cucumbers. As the experiment was repeated each day for a week, the anomalous day stands out as a "glitch." That trial still needs to be recorded and analyzed, but its effect on the conclusion is less pronounced.

Similarly, the best way to deal with biological variation is to increase the number of people, animals, or plants studied. Imagine an economic experiment designed to test if brand-name jeans last longer than generic jeans when worn by boys in the first grade. Special emphasis will be placed on the survival of the fabric in the knee region. The differences between boys will undoubtedly be greater than the differences between fabrics. Some boys are more active than others. The types of activities will also vary, some will be kneelers, some will be sitters, and some will be runners and/or fallers. One way to circumvent this problem is to test lots and lots of boys. If there are enough boys in each group, the differences between boys will "average out." In other words, on the average, each group will contain about the same number of active and not-so-active boys.

Human error is always a factor in experiments. Care and skill can minimize this source of variation, but it will always affect the data. Another experiment is designed to test if iron-on or sew-on patches last longer when used to mend little boy's jeans. The adhesive on the iron-on patches may be affected, for example, by small variations in the temperature of the iron. Even if the experimenters are taking care to be as consistent as possible, small variations in iron temperature may have noticeable effects. Similarly, the length of the stitches used to attach the patch may affect the longevity of the sew-on variety. Experimenters sewing patches by hand will not be able to produce absolutely uniform stitches for every patch. The best results will be obtained by increasing the sample size. If enough patches are analyzed, small differences in the way the patches were attached to the jeans, will again "average out."

What about experiments that just do not "work"? These are not experiments that proved that the model was incorrect. These are experiments that produce inconclusive data or no data. What does the experimenter do now? *If at first you don't succeed, try, try again—but first think about what went wrong.* What can be changed to improve the experiment? I tried most of the experiments discussed in this book. Not all of them worked the first time, but I sometimes learned valuable information from the "failures." From the apple browning experiment in Chapter 7, I learned that tart, green apples do not turn brown even when they are exposed to air for a long time. When testing the stain solubility experiment in Chapter 4, I learned that the ink in ballpoint pens is not soluble in water. (Ballpoint pens are therefore useful for labeling the coffee filters.) The first time I did the bean seedling experiment (Chapter 4 and Appendix 2), only one bean grew, so I repeated the experiment with four times as many seeds. A failed experiment is not the end of the world. A failed experiment can provide an opportunity to learn. Children may be disappointed when their experiment does not yield analyzable data. Try brainstorming to come up with new approaches to the experiment. Positive controls are particularly useful for troubleshooting unsuccessful experiments and for identifying which step in an experiment may have failed.

Remember the following points:

- Have fun with the experiment. Experiments are an opportunity to learn, not an intelligence test. Everyone makes mistakes. Smart people learn from them.
- Careful planning ensures that the experiment can be done easily and safely. The use of controls simplifies data analysis. Be certain that the experiment is testing only one thing at a time.
- A good laboratory notebook aids in both the performance of the experiment and the analysis of the data. Advance planning helps ensure that the

experiment will proceed smoothly. Discovering that vital information was omitted from the laboratory notebook is disappointing. Making that discovery on the night before the science fair is devastating. Review the notebook and analyze the data while there is still time to repeat the experiment.

- A failed experiment can be fixed. Positive controls help identify flaws in experimental design.

- Good laboratory technique is an asset, but mistakes will occur. Repeating an experiment provides an opportunity to improve it.

- There will be variability in the data from every experiment. Glitches are okay. The experiment may simply have to be repeated with more trials or samples.

- The data are telling you something. If the data prove that the model is incorrect, then further research may be necessary. If the experiment did not "work," there must be a reason. Try brainstorming to come up with possible explanations and alternative experiments.

N O T E

1. Prepare a blank table before starting the experiment. List all of the experimental treatments, and leave ample space to record the data. The experimenters can simply fill in the blanks as they do the experiment.

6

What Does It Mean?

Data Analysis & Presentation

Do not worry about your difficulties in mathematics: I can assure you that mine are still greater.

—*Albert Einstein*

SCIENTIFIC INFORMATION IS OFTEN COMPILED IN GRAPHS AND TABLES BECAUSE these formats help experimenters organize and understand their data. Graphing is a powerful analytical tool because it allows the visualization of numerical data. Creating and examining graphs, therefore, often leads to new insights into the data and the experiment. Preparing tables organizes numeric and non-numeric results in a way that emphasizes the appropriate comparisons, and facilitates drawing the correct conclusions. Graphing and tabulating data are important components of the scientific problem-solving toolkit.

Scientific tables and graphs also help experimenters present their data. Students gain deeper insight into their science projects as they explain the experiments to others. In order to present the experimental results, students must challenge their assumptions about the experiment, and determine the simplest and clearest way to explain the data. Selecting the best format for data presentation is critical to communicating ideas and information.

Number crunching

Many experiments are designed to yield numeric data. The results of the sledding experiment were the number of seconds required for each sled to go down the hill. The bean seedling experiment (Chapter 4 and Appendix 2) yielded the heights of the bean plants measured in inches. There may be many numbers to analyze, especially if the experiment was done with replicate measurements. *Number crunching* is sorting, analyzing, and understanding numerical data.

The first consideration in number crunching is the mathematical ability of the experimenters. Replicate observations cannot be averaged if the experimenters have not yet learned division, and standard statistical calculations are inappropriate for elementary school students. Statistics are usually not necessary for children's science, and correct conclusions can be reached without them. Children can gain an understanding of concepts like experimental error and the differences between groups of numbers through visual examination of graphs and tables.

Experimental error is part of life in science. The concept of experimental error was introduced in Chapter 5, and the suggested remedy was making replicate observations. Replicate measurements rarely yield identical values. Sometimes repeated measurements vary over a wide range, and the ranges of two groups of numbers may overlap. Here is the dilemma: how can you tell if two sets of numbers are really different? How do you know, for example, which sled is really the fastest? How do you know if bean seedlings grow faster in forest loam or commercial potting soil?

Graph the data. A picture is worth a thousand words.

What is a graph? A graph is a picture of numerical data: a 2-dimensional representation of an experiment. The vertical (*y*) axis corresponds to what was measured or observed in the experiment. The horizontal (*x*) axis corresponds to what was varied in the experiment.[1] To plot the weights of the sleds used in the sledding experiment, the weights are shown on the vertical axis, and the type of sled is shown on the horizontal axis. (Figure 6.1.) To plot the growth of a bean plant, the height of the plant is shown on the vertical axis, and the number of days after planting is shown on the horizontal axis. (Figure 6.2.) The most common types of graphs used to represent scientific data are bar graphs and line graphs. Pie charts are rarely used in science, although they can be useful to express fractions for children who have not yet learned division. Histograms have scientific applications, but for children's experiments a bar graph will usually suffice. Bar graphs are used when the variables plotted on the horizontal (x) axis are not directly related to each other, or they are not numeric. For example, when graphing the weights of the sleds used in the sledding experiment, the different sleds are independent of each other, they are not numerically related, in fact, they are not numbers. The data are therefore plotted on a bar graph. (Figure 6.1.) Line graphs are used when the variables plotted on the horizontal (x) axis change in relationship to each other. For example, when plotting bean seedling growth vs. days after planting, a line graph should be used. The days after planting represent a progression of numbers because the height of a bean plant on day 8 is numerically related to its height on day 7. (Figure 6.2.) Line graphs are often used to depict how things change with time or in relation to altering a variable in the experiment.

Label the axes of the graph. Near the vertical axis, write what was measured, and include the units. Was the sled speed measured in milliseconds, seconds, minutes, years, or millennia? Near the horizontal axis, write what was varied. Include the units, if appropriate. When several treatments or conditions are used, a legend is necessary to identify them. For example, in one of the bar graphs for the sledding experiment (Figure 6.4b), the bars denoting

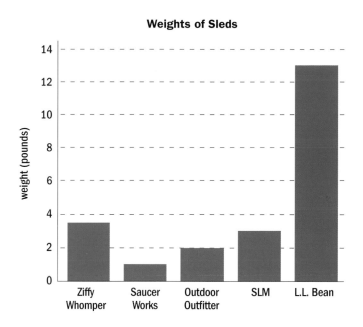

Figure 6.1. Weights of Sleds. The Saucer Works sled is the lightest sled used in this experiment. The L. L. Bean sled is 13 times heavier than the Saucer Works sled.

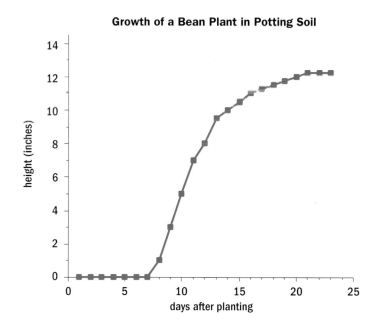

Figure 6.2. Growth of a Bean Plant in Potting Soil. Bean plants grow rapidly in potting soil. This plant was 1 inch tall on the 8th day after planting, and reached its maximum height of 12½ inches by the 21st day.

the sleds were differentiated by color and identified in the legend. Remember to put a title on the graph explaining what was measured in the experiment. A graph should tell a comprehensible, self-explanatory story about an experiment.

Children may need some help to plot the data, but graphing is something children enjoy. Seeing the data in graphical form often helps scientists of all ages to understand their experiments. In plotting the data by hand, the students must think about what they are doing, and what the data mean.[2] Provide appropriate guidance and assistance with graphing. Help decide which type of graph should be used. Next, have the children set up the two axes, complete with values and units on graph paper.

For a bar graph, the x-axis should be labeled at regular intervals identifying what was varied in the experiment. In Figure 6.1, the labels on the x-axis indicate the specific sleds. In this graph, the y-axis refers to the weights of the sleds. For each particular sled, the children must locate its weight in pounds on the y-axis, and draw a bar of the appropriate height. (The sled weights could also be presented in a table as they were in Chapter 3.)

For a line graph, both the x- and y-axes represent a numerical progression, often a linear scale. When plotting the growth of a bean plant, the horizontal axis indicates what was varied in the experiment, or the number of days after planting the seeds. The vertical axis denotes what was measured, or the growth of the bean plant. (Figure 6.2). Each data point is represented by two numbers, the height of the plant, and the number of days after planting, so students must find the point on the grid that corresponds to each pair of numbers. For example, they must match 1 inch of plant height with day 8, 3 inches with day 9, and 5 inches with day 10. When all of the points in a data set are plotted, the dots are connected.

Experimental Error Revisited

How do graphs help scientists cope with experimental error? Table 6.1 shows two groups of numbers. Imagine that they represent the spelling test scores of left-handed and right-handed children in a third grade class. On the average, numbers in the left-handed group are larger than the numbers in the right-handed group, but the two groups of numbers overlap. Are the two groups really

Table 6.1. Spelling Scores of Left- and Right-handed Children

LEFT-HANDED	RIGHT-HANDED
10	8
8	7
6	3
12	6
AVERAGE = 9	AVERAGE = 6

different? Can we conclude that left-handed children are better spellers (or at least did better on this test) than right-handed children? Try plotting the data.

Individual and average spelling test scores are shown in Figure 6.3a and 6.3b. The graph of the individual values demonstrates the overlap between the two groups. The left-handed group has two high points, and the right-handed group has one low point, but there is little difference between the remaining numbers in the groups. The conclusion from this graph is that while the left-handed group has a couple of students who did well on this test, the left-handers are not consistently better at spelling than the right-handers. The two groups are not really different.

Now look at the average values. The average score for the left-handed group is 9, while the average score for the right-handed group is 6. Most people would agree that 9 is greater than 6. When only the average values are considered, the obvious although incorrect conclusion is that left-handed students know this spelling lesson better than the right-handed students. The danger of expressing data as averages in the absence of formal statistics is that glitches may be overemphasized. A single low point reduces an average, even if that low point represents an experimental fluke (or a child who was ill when he took the exam). By graphing all of the data, the overall performance of a group is evident.

If adult scientists were plotting the data in Table 6.1, they would use average values, but the scatter within each group would be represented with standard error bars, the T- or I-shaped markings seen in professional graphs. Scientists would

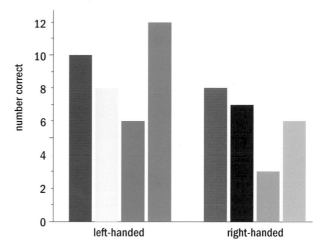

Figure 6.3a. The individual spelling test scores of left-handed and right-handed students overlap.

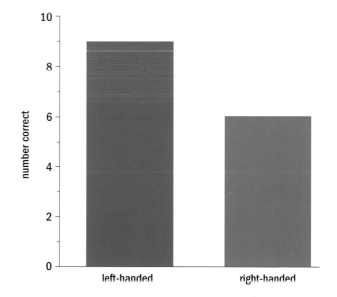

Figure 6.3b. The average spelling test score of left-handed students is higher than that of right-handed students.

express the difference between the two groups of children as a statistical probability. Statistics are a valuable tool, but elementary school students can not handle the math. Statistics are not usually necessary for children to draw the correct conclusions from their data. The best way to cope with experimental error is to face up to it. Plot all of the points, and observe how the scatter in the data affects the outcome. A single outlying point may not alter the overall conclusion. Significant overlap between two sets of numbers usually implies that the two groups are not different.

Graphs can help explain the data.

Table 6.2. Sled Run Times

		RUN TIMES	
SLED	#1	#2	#3
Ziffy Whomper	10.17	10.97	9.38
Saucer Works	8.07	5.96	7.42
Outdoor Outfitter	13.37	9.50	8.90
SLM	14.37	11.09	8.93
L. L. Bean	11.41	11.30	9.90

How should the sledding experiment be graphed? The sled run times are shown in Table 6.2, and plotted in three different ways in Figure 6.4a, b, c.

My first idea was to plot the data in a bar graph as shown in Figure 6.4a. I assumed that the data points were independent of each other, so a bar graph seemed to be a good choice. The data are grouped by the type of sled. This graph clearly demonstrates that the Saucer Works sled is the fastest under the conditions tested. The run times of the Saucer Works sled do not overlap with the run times of any other sled. In fact, the slowest Saucer Works time is a second faster than any other sled. Observe that the heavy L. L. Bean sled is not the slowest. Furthermore, this bar graph indicates that the sledding track was getting faster as the experiment progressed. Note the downward trend in each group of three bars. Figure 6.4b is a second bar graph in which the data are grouped by run number. Arranging the data in this way facilitates its analysis because the speed of the track increased as the experiment progressed. This graph emphasizes the comparison of sled runs done in similar snow conditions. The Saucer Works sled is the fastest in every snow condition

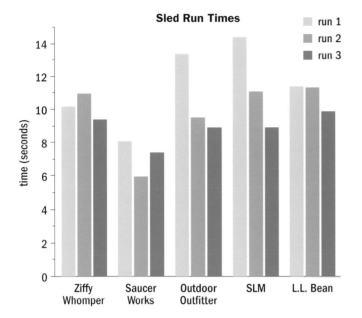

Figure 6.4a. Grouping the sled run times by the type of sled demonstrates that the Saucer Works sled is the fastest, and the L. L. Bean sled is not the slowest. The downward sloping trend of each group of three runs indicates that the sled track was getting faster with successive runs.

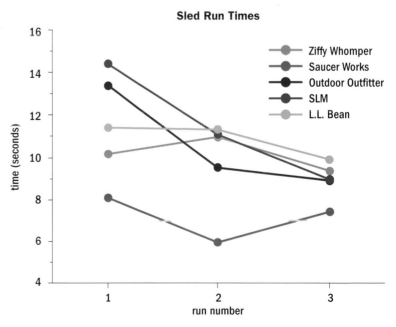

Figure 6.4b. Grouping the sled run times by run number achieves a more objective evaluation. Each sled run is compared to other runs done in similar snow conditions.

Figure 6.4c. A line graph clearly demonstrates that the Saucer Works sled is the fastest in all snow conditions tested. This graph emphasizes the effect of snow condition on all of the sleds tested.

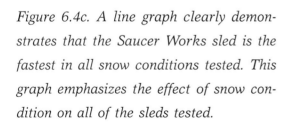

tested. Lizzy, the girl who did the sledding experiment, and her father suggested making a line graph (Figure 6.4c). The line graph is a reasonable approach because the sled runs do, in fact, represent a numerical progression. Each successive sled run packs the snow more firmly and makes the track faster. The line graph demonstrates several points.

1. The Saucer Works sled won by a mile (or at least by 1½ seconds in every snow condition tested).
2. When the snow was packed, all the sleds except the Saucer Works sled completed the run in about the same time (approximately 9 seconds).
3. The type of sled made a big difference (more than 6 seconds) in the initial runs when the snow was powder.
4. The speeds of the SLM sled and the Outdoor Outfitter sled were most affected by snow condition. (The slopes of these lines are the steepest.)
5. The heavy L. L. Bean Sled was not significantly slower than the other sleds.

Graphs help experimenters understand and interpret their data, and provide visual representations that allow a clearer presentation of the data to others. Different types of graphs emphasize different ideas, so employing several different graphing techniques helps ensure that all of the available information has been extracted from the data. Thorough data analysis using several types of graphs may reveal unexpected conclusions.

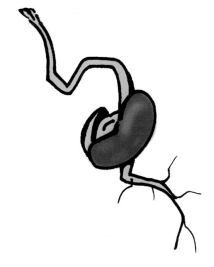

Graphs produced from the bean seedling growth experiment are shown in Figures 6.5, 6.6, 6.7, and 6.8. Figure 6.7 represents all of the data collected in this experiment. Figures 6.5, 6.6, and 6.8 emphasize particular aspects of the experiment (sprouting time, number of seeds that germinated, and final plant height).

The time required for the bean sprouts to appear above the soil is shown in Figure 6.5. Sprouts were observed between the 4th and 14th days after planting. Bean seeds planted in forest loam and potting soil or germinated on damp paper towels sprouted within the same time period (on or before the 11th day). The bean seeds planted in sand required more time to reach the surface of the soil (13–14 days).

The number of seeds that germinated in each soil type is shown in Figure 6.6. These data can be expressed as fractions or percentages if the experimenters understand those mathematical concepts. For younger students, pictorial representations may

Figure 6.5. Appearance of Sprouts. Sprouts appeared between the 4th and 14th day after planting. The number of sprouts that appeared on a given day is indicated by the height of the bar and the color indicates the type of soil. Seeds planted in potting soil and forest loam or germinated on damp paper towels, sprouted on or before the 11th day. Seeds planted in sand did not sprout until the 13th and 14th days. The seeds germinated on paper towels were counted as sprouting when the shoots grew 1 inch from the seed because the seeds grown in soil were planted about 1 inch beneath the surface.

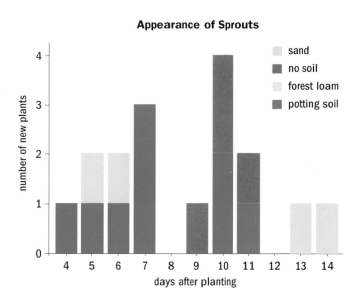

illustrate the concept more clearly. Twelve bean seeds were planted in each soil type. In potting soil, nine of the twelve seeds (75%) grew into plants. In forest loam and sand, only two of the twelve seeds (17%) sprouted. Of the six seeds germinated on damp paper towels, four (67%) grew into bean plants.

The growth rate of the bean plants is illustrated in Figure 6.7. The beans planted in forest loam and potting soil or germinated on damp paper towels grow at the same rate, and attain about the

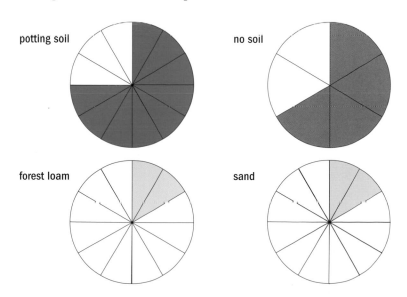

Number of Beans That Sprouted in Different Soils

Colored segments indicate beans that germinated.
White segments indicate beans that did not germinate.

Figure 6.6. The Number of Beans That Sprouted in Different Soils. Nine of the twelve seeds planted in potting soil germinated. Four of the six seeds incubated on damp paper towels sprouted. Two of the twelve seeds planted in forest loam grew into plants. Two of the twelve seeds planted in sand sprouted.

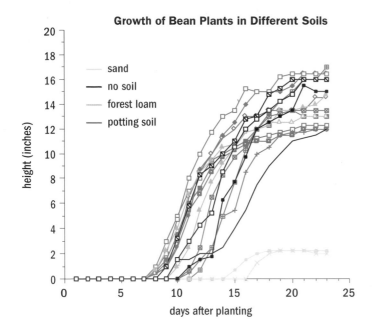

Figure 6.7. Growth of Bean Plants in Different Soils. The slopes of the lines indicate the growth rate of bean plants, and steeper slopes imply faster growth rates. Bean seeds planted in potting soil and forest loam and seeds germinated on damp paper towels grew at the same rate. Seeds planted in sand grew at similar or slightly slower rates.

same heights. (Compare black, red, and green lines.) The beans planted in sand (blue lines) did not grow as well as the other plants. Bean seedlings planted in sand stopped growing when they reached 2 inches in height. The other plants grew to be 12 to 17 inches high. (See Figure 6.8.) These growth defects were not caused by a lack of nutrients in the sand because the no-soil controls grew as rapidly and as tall as the beans planted in potting soil. Bean seeds apparently contain enough nutrients to support plant growth until leaves develop and photosynthesis can occur.

Figure 6.8. Heights of Bean Plants 23 Days After Planting. Bean seeds planted in potting soil and forest loam and seeds germinated on damp paper towels grew to similar heights (12 to 17 inches). Bean plants grown in sand did not exceed 2 inches in height.

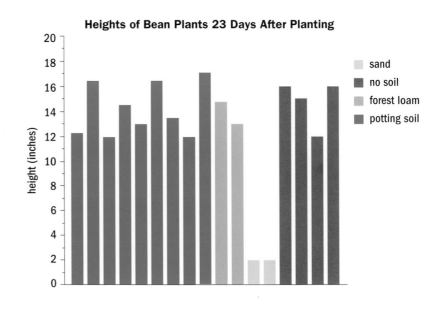

Returning to the original experimental question, do bean plants grow faster when planted in commercial potting soil, forest loam, or sand? The four graphs produced from this experiment answer the question and provide additional information.

1. Beans planted in potting soil, forest loam, or on damp paper towels germinated by the 11th day. Beans planted in sand sprouted later on the 13th and 14th days.

2. Bean plants grew from nine of the twelve seeds planted in potting soil, two of the twelve seeds planted in sand or forest loam, and four of the six seeds germinated on damp paper towels.

3. Bean plants grew at the same rate in potting soil, forest loam, and without soil. (The slopes of the lines in Figure 6.7 are the same.) The growth rate of beans planted in sand is slightly slower or similar to the growth rates of the other plants.

4. Bean plants grown in potting soil and forest loam or germinated on damp paper towels attained similar heights (12–17 inches). Beans planted in sand produced plants that stopped growing at a height of 2 inches.

Non-numeric data (Qualitative Analysis)

Not every experiment yields numeric data. The penny brightening experiment (Chapter 4), the sock washing experiment (Chapter 4), and the apple browning experiment (Chapter 7) all produce qualitative data. The experimental samples can be ranked in comparison to controls, but numbers are not involved. Analyzing and presenting this type of data requires a different approach.

Non-numeric data can be presented in tabular form, or as photographs or drawings. To compile Table 6.3, dirty socks washed in different detergents were ranked for relative cleanliness, and compared to the positive and

Table 6.3. Comparison of the Cleaning Power of Two Detergents

TREATMENT	SCORE	SCORE	SCORE	SCORE
New socks	++++	++++	++++	++++
Washed in brand A	++	+	++	+
Washed in brand B	+++	+++	+++	+++
Not washed	–	–	–	–
Washed in water alone	+/–	+/–	–	+

Table 6.4. Adding Descriptions to Table 6.3

TREATMENT	SCORE	SCORE	SCORE	SCORE	DESCRIPTION
New socks	++++	++++	++++	++++	Bright white
Washed in brand A	++	+	++	+	Gray with darker spots
Washed in brand B	+++	+++	+++	+++	White, but not as bright as new socks
Not washed	–	–	–	–	Dark gray to black
Washed in water alone	+/–	+/–	–	+	Dark gray

negative controls. A score of "–" was given to unwashed socks, and "+ + + +" awarded to new socks.

A certain amount of subjectivity involved in compiling this type of table. Encourage children to be as honest as possible when comparing the experimental samples to their controls. Objectivity can be improved by using a "blind" analysis in which the evaluator does not know which socks belong to which group. In blind analyses, creative labeling is necessary to keep track of the socks. In the apple browning experiment, objectivity was assured by having the entire classroom judge each treatment. While a few students may have been prejudiced in favor of the treatment that they suggested, the others were expected to be unbiased.

Another way to enhance objectivity is to compare the samples to a standard. I originally thought that paint chips could provide an objective reference for the apple browning experiment. I discovered, however, that paint chips are not manufactured in the shades produced in apple browning. (The hues of muddy socks may be more popular house paint colors.) In any case, the best comparisons are to the positive and negative controls.

Experimental error must be considered in non-numeric experiments, so replicates are important. As with numeric data, show all of the data points. Consider the overlap between the data sets, and observe if any data set is unique. The data in Table 6.3 demonstrate that brand B gets the socks cleaner than brand A. In one trial, washing with plain water got the socks as clean as washing with brand A. Washing the socks with plain water usually, but not always, partially cleaned the socks.

Descriptive phrases can be useful additions to a table. Ranking the socks as "gray soles with darker spots" provides more information than +/–. Other information such as noting that one of the detergents turned the socks yellow or ate holes in the socks can be included in a table of this kind. Descriptions can be mentioned in footnotes, or in a separate column of the table.

Photographs are useful in qualitative analyses because they give the audience an opportunity to judge the data for themselves. Photographs of the apple slices or washed socks would clearly demonstrate the results. Results can also be sketched, if care is taken to maintain objectivity. Photographs or sketches greatly enhance the appeal of the final presentation.

What was learned?

Did the experiment answer the question?

1. The sledding experiment demonstrated that the Saucer Works sled is definitely the fastest. The data also suggest that the Saucer Works sled is the fastest because it has the smoothest bottom (model 1). Sled weight (model 2) appears to be less important in determining sled speed because the heaviest sled was not the slowest. The effect of color on sled speed (model 3) was not rigorously tested in this experiment.

2. The data from the bean growth experiment indicate that planting beans in potting soil produces good results for the four criteria tested: germination time, percent of planted seeds that sprout, growth rate, and final height. Similar growth rates, germination times, and final heights were observed with beans planted in forest loam, but fewer seeds sprouted in forest loam. Planting seeds in sand produced the poorest results. Beans germinated without soil do as well as beans planted in potting soil, however these plants do not have straight stems, and they require more care as the paper towels must be moistened each day.

3. The sock washing experiment demonstrates that brand B is the best buy in laundry detergent. The cost of brand B is lower, and the socks washed in this detergent become cleaner than those washed in brand A.

Is it right?

The bean growth, sledding and washing detergent experiments all produced believable data, although the poor performance of the seedlings planted in sand was surprising. Unexpected results may require the formulation of a new model.

Did the experiment demonstrate other interesting information?

1. The effect of snow condition on sled speed was additional useful information. The S.L.M. and Outdoor Outfitter sleds were more affected by snow conditions than the other sleds.

2. There is something about sand that inhibits bean seedling growth. The sand used in this experiment was intended for use in children's sandboxes, so this sand may have been treated with chemicals that prevent weed growth. Another explanation for the poor performance of bean seeds in sand may be the lack of aeration in tightly packed soil. Commercial potting soil contains vermiculite to improve soil aeration. Adding vermiculite to forest loam or sand may improve these soils for bean plant growth.

3. Washing the socks in plain water is not an effective method for removing mud.

Data presentation: Posters

How do you show the world (or the other participants in the science fair) the results of your careful planning, hard work, and analytical thinking? Construct a scientific poster. This type of presentation has several advantages. Children do not have to perform a successful demonstration in front of an audience. The poster provides "crib notes" so that the experimenter can easily refer to previously determined conclusions. Graphs, pictures or photographs are available to demonstrate results and conclusions to the audience. A poster should be complete and self-explanatory so people viewing the poster can read the information at their own pace and formulate questions for the presenter.

What should go on the poster?

1. The title of the poster can be the question that the experiment was intended to answer, or the major conclusion of the experiment. ("Which Sled Is The Fastest?" or "The Saucer Works Sled Is The Fastest.")

2. The names of the experimenters.

3. An abstract (optional). Concise summaries of experiments are often difficult to write, but abstracts quickly introduce the experiment to the audience. Consider using a simple format. "Question: Which sled is the fastest? Model: The Saucer Works sled is the fastest because it has the smoothest bottom. Conclusion: The Saucer Works Sled is the fastest sled in all conditions tested."

4. The model. State the model that the experiment was designed to test.

5. The method. Explain how the experiment was done, including consistency considerations and controls.

6. The results. Include graphs, tables, photographs, and/or drawings. Every figure should have a legend explaining the conclusions of the graph, or table, or what the photograph or sketch illustrates.

7. The conclusions. List what was learned from the experiment. Note individual conclusions with numbers or bullets. Use large, legible type.

8. Acknowledgements. Any special assistance obtained for planning or performing the experiment should be acknowledged on the poster.

9. Photographs of the experiment in progress (optional). Photographs of the children sledding down the hill, measuring the bean seedlings, or preparing the dirty socks add interest to poster presentations.

The poster is the culmination of a large amount of work and thought by the children. They should be proud of their efforts, and this pride can be reflected in a beautiful poster. Be certain that the writing is legible, and that the letters are large and dark enough to be read by people standing a few feet away. The graphs should be clearly labeled. All figures should include a clearly written legend. The poster should completely explain the experimental model, methods, results, and conclusions.

What's next?

The answers to scientific inquiries often lead to more questions. The problem-solving method diagramed in Figure 1.1 is cyclic. An arrow extends from "Answer or Conclusion" back to "Question." The scientific process can be viewed perhaps more accurately as an endless spiral. Each experiment is designed to answer a question, but the answer invariably generates new questions. Scientific projects rarely end. They evolve and change, but the process of asking, experimenting, learning, and asking other questions continues. This inquiring attitude and unlimited curiosity is the core of the learning process, and precisely why children are so much like scientists.

To a scientist thinking about the *next* experiment is one of the most exciting parts of the scientific method. This is the thrill of the chase. Marie Curie said, "One never notices what has been done; one can only see what remains to be done."

Applying the scientific method to one problem leads inexorably to more questions, new challenges, and more experiments.

Children who are intensely involved in a scientific investigation often wish to follow up on their interests with additional experiments. Time and scheduling considerations may prevent extensive further experimentation, but providing closure to a project is often helpful. A speculative brainstorming session about possible future experiments may be satisfactory, or additional experiments can be planned and performed. For example, one student might suggest testing if his new red, *metal* saucer sled is as fast as the lighter red, *plastic* saucer sled. In this case, the color and the shape of the two sleds are the same, but the metal one is much heavier. For the bean seedling experiment, the students may be wondering what happened to the beans that never sprouted. Most of the beans placed on the damp paper towels germinated. What happened to the beans that did not come up in the sand and forest loam? An "autopsy" performed on the unsprouted seeds indicated that the seeds decayed. The unsprouted seeds in forest loam grew pale green mold, and became soft and mushy. The unsprouted seeds in sand turned purplish pink, soft, and mushy. Not all of the planted bean seeds could be found, presumably because they decomposed during the three-week experiment.

The follow up experiments need not be complicated and time consuming. The bean autopsy required only a few minutes to perform and analyze. Unlike adult scientists, school children cannot pursue their scientific interests at the expense of other subjects, but their curiosity can often be encouraged with a small experiment or a short discussion.

Suggestions for understanding your data.

1. For numeric data, plot all of the data points. Young children will better understand their experiment if the data points are not averaged.
2. Analyze the samples in non-numeric experiments as honestly as possible. Blind analyses may be useful.
3. Observe whether the data sets overlap. Is there a logical explanation for outlying points? Is one set clearly different from the others?
4. Has the experiment answered the question?
5. Did the data provide additional unexpected information?

The Sledding Experiment

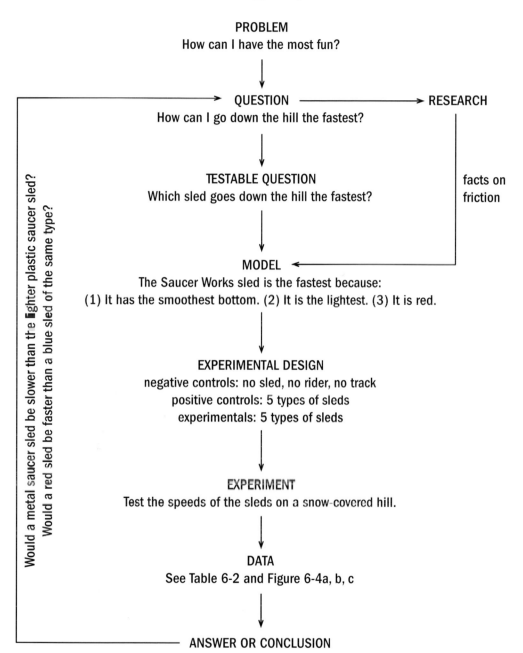

PROBLEM
How can I have the most fun?

QUESTION ──────────→ **RESEARCH**
How can I go down the hill the fastest?

facts on
friction

TESTABLE QUESTION
Which sled goes down the hill the fastest?

MODEL ◄──────────
The Saucer Works sled is the fastest because:
(1) It has the smoothest bottom. (2) It is the lightest. (3) It is red.

EXPERIMENTAL DESIGN
negative controls: no sled, no rider, no track
positive controls: 5 types of sleds
experimentals: 5 types of sleds

EXPERIMENT
Test the speeds of the sleds on a snow-covered hill.

DATA
See Table 6-2 and Figure 6-4a, b, c

Would a metal saucer sled be slower than the lighter plastic saucer sled?
Would a red sled be faster than a blue sled of the same type?

ANSWER OR CONCLUSION
The Saucer Works sled is the fastest sled in all snow conditions tested. The heaviest
sled (L.L. Bean) is not the slowest, so the speed of the Saucer Works sled is probably
due to the smooth bottom of the sled. Sled color was not tested in this experiment.

Figure 6.9. Flow Chart of the Sledding Experiment.

The Bean Seedling Experiment

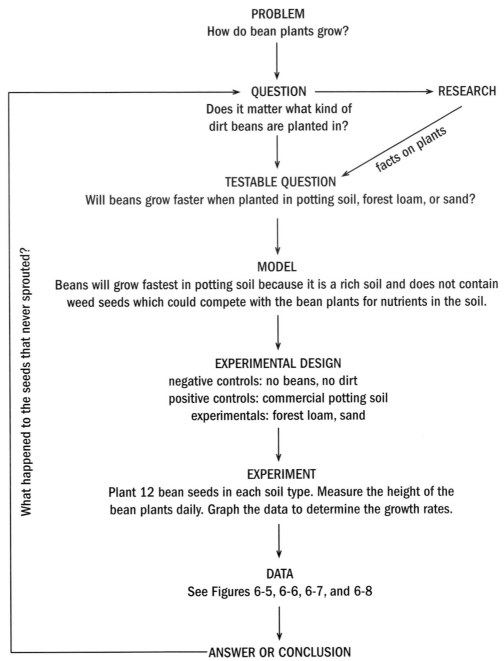

PROBLEM
How do bean plants grow?

QUESTION ———→ RESEARCH
Does it matter what kind of
dirt beans are planted in?

facts on plants

TESTABLE QUESTION
Will beans grow faster when planted in potting soil, forest loam, or sand?

MODEL
Beans will grow fastest in potting soil because it is a rich soil and does not contain
weed seeds which could compete with the bean plants for nutrients in the soil.

EXPERIMENTAL DESIGN
negative controls: no beans, no dirt
positive controls: commercial potting soil
experimentals: forest loam, sand

EXPERIMENT
Plant 12 bean seeds in each soil type. Measure the height of the
bean plants daily. Graph the data to determine the growth rates.

DATA
See Figures 6-5, 6-6, 6-7, and 6-8

ANSWER OR CONCLUSION
Potting soil is the best medium for bean growth. The seeds planted in forest loam
germinated within the same time period, grew at the same rate, and attained similar
heights as the seeds planted in potting soil, but fewer seeds sprouted. Growing
seeds in sand produced poorer results than growing seeds in the absence of soil.

What happened to the seeds that never sprouted?

Figure 6.10. Flow Chart of the Bean Seedling Experiment.

Which Detergent Gets Dirty Socks the Cleanest?

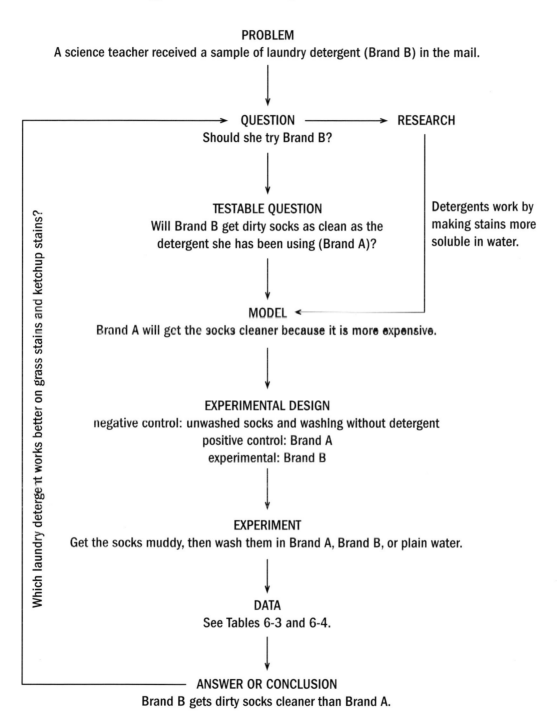

PROBLEM
A science teacher received a sample of laundry detergent (Brand B) in the mail.

QUESTION ———————→ RESEARCH
Should she try Brand B?

Detergents work by making stains more soluble in water.

TESTABLE QUESTION
Will Brand B get dirty socks as clean as the detergent she has been using (Brand A)?

MODEL
Brand A will get the socks cleaner because it is more expensive.

EXPERIMENTAL DESIGN
negative control: unwashed socks and washing without detergent
positive control: Brand A
experimental: Brand B

EXPERIMENT
Get the socks muddy, then wash them in Brand A, Brand B, or plain water.

DATA
See Tables 6-3 and 6-4.

ANSWER OR CONCLUSION
Brand B gets dirty socks cleaner than Brand A.

Which laundry detergent works better on grass stains and ketchup stains?

Figure 6.11. Flow Chart of the Sock Washing Experiment.

6. Prepare a legible, well-organized, self-explanatory poster.

7. Are future experiments indicated?

The brains-on approach to science was outlined in Chapter 1, and explained in subsequent chapters. The diagrams in Figures 6.9, 6.10, and 6.11 show how the brains-on method was used to plan and perform the sledding, bean seedling, and sock washing experiments.

N O T E S

1. The terms "dependent variable" for the *y*-axis, and "independent variable" for the *x*-axis are sometimes used. The measured values plotted on the *y*-axis *depend* on what was varied in the experiment.

2. Computer graphing programs can also be useful as they facilitate graphing, make beautiful pictures, and make it easier to plot the data in several different ways. Be certain that the children who produce computer-generated graphs have taken the time to think about what the graph means. Using a computer should not substitute for thinking.

Examples of

Experiments

You will do foolish things, but do them with enthusiasm.

—Colette

THE EXPERIMENTS DISCUSSED IN THIS CHAPTER WERE DERIVED FROM QUES-tions asked by young children. Each experiment was chosen to illustrate specific concepts of the brains-on method. "Is money the dirtiest stuff around?" demonstrates how to refine and clarify a question. "How does the remote control on the TV work?" exemplifies the need for researching the experimental subject. "Why is apple cider brown?" illustrates the importance of experimental controls. "How do you make a parachute for a Beanie Baby?" emphasizes data analysis.

Is money the dirtiest object around?

Let's consider the question "Is money the dirtiest object around?" What kind of money are we talking about?

- *Coins.*
- *Dollar bills.*
- *Credit cards.*

Well, those are all types of money. I think though, to be on the safe side, we should probably use coins in our experiment. Some of the treatments might damage paper money or credit cards. What do you mean by dirty?

- *It has dirt on it.*
- *Or germs.*

Okay, so you're saying that "dirty" can mean covered with dirt or germs. Would you like to investigate both meanings in our experiment? We can divide the class into two groups: the dirt group and the germ group. Let's start with dirt. What do you think "the dirtiest object around" means? Around what?

- *Around here or around the house.*

Okay, so is money dirtier than a pebble from the playground?

- *No. It doesn't look dirtier.*

Shall we test that? The pebble on the playground will be my suggestion. Can you tell me some other things that might be dirtier than money?

- *A stick from the swamp.*
- *The bottom of my shoe.*
- *A dead mouse.*
- *Ooh, gross!*

I wrote down "a pebble from the playground, a stick from the swamp, the bottom of Kelly's shoe, and a dead mouse." Any comments?

- *A dead mouse is gross.*
- *Where are you going to get one anyway?*
- *I don't know—just somewhere.*

I think in the interest of health concerns we probably can't test the dead mouse. Are their any comments about the other suggestions? No? Okay. We'll test them. How are we going to tell how dirty something is?

- *Wash it and see if it gets cleaner.*
- *Then we'll have a bunch of clean stuff. We won't know how dirty it was to start with.*
- *We could see how much dirt comes off in the water.*
- *We could compare the water from washing all the dirty things and see which is the dirtiest.*

How are we going to tell which wash water is the dirtiest?

- *Look at it, and see which is the darkest or the most cloudy.*
- *Some of the dirt will sink to the bottom.*

I was thinking we could filter the wash water through white coffee filters, and then see which coffee filter is the dirtiest.

- *Okay. How are we going to wash the stuff?*
- *We could shake the things in a jar of soapy water.*
- *My shoe won't fit in a jar.*
- *We'll use a dishpan for your shoe.*

So, first we have to gather up all the dirty things we need: a coin, a pebble, the stick, and the shoe. We'll wash them by shaking them in soapy water. The wash water will be filtered through coffee filters, and we'll compare the filters and see which is dirtiest. Any comments on experimental consistency?

- *We should use the same amount of water to wash everything.*
- *We should use the same amount and kind of soap for everything.*
- *We should wash everything the same amount.*
- *You mean for the same time. We could shake everything in the water for the same amount of time.*

Good ideas! Are there any other comments?

- *The shoe is bigger than the other things. It can hold more dirt.*

I hadn't thought of that. Do we need to be consistent about the size of the dirty object?

- *How are we going to make the shoe smaller?*
- *We could just wash part of the shoe.*
- *How are we going to do that?*
- *We could just wash the toe or the heel.*
- *We could use shoes with high heels. It would be easy to wash the heel separately from the rest of the shoe.*
- *We also need to find a swamp stick that is about the same size as the coin.*

Good ideas! What are the controls for this experiment?

[No response.]

Do you remember from the sledding experiment that a positive control is something that we know will work? What would positively make the wash water dirty?

- *A positive control could be washing plain dirt. We could put a dirt clod in the wash water and filter it.*

Good. Can anyone think of a negative control? A negative control is something that isn't supposed to work. Remember in the sledding experiment, the negative controls were no sled, no rider, or no track. What could we leave out of this experiment to ensure that what we observe is caused by the experimental treatment?

- *We could leave out the dirty thing. We could filter plain soapy water.*

Excellent. I can see that this class understands the importance of experimental controls. Let's move on to germs. Does money have more germs on it than other things?

- *You can't see germs. How can we tell if there are germs on money?*
- *We could look at the coins with a microscope, and look for germs.*
- *We don't have a microscope.*
- *What does a germ look like anyway?[1]*

This is a tough one, but I have some ideas about germs. We can't see a single germ with our eyes, but we can see a large group or "colony" of them. Has anyone seen a colony of green or black mold on bread or white mold on cheese? We could test if microorganisms are on a coin by letting them grow and multiply until they become a colony that is big enough to see. When I was in school, we grew microorganisms on solid medium in Petri plates. The solid medium looked a lot like brown Jell-O. The Petri plates are little plastic dishes that hold solid media, and have lids that prevent germs in the air from contaminating the experiment. I have a recipe for making solid medium in canning jars. I could make up the medium at home, and bring it in. You could test money and other things for germs. What would you like to test?

- *My tongue.*
- *My fingers.*
- *The heel of the shoe.*
- *The stick from the swamp.*
- *It's too bad we can't test the dead mouse.*

I wrote down "a coin, Justin's tongue, Sara's fingers, a shoe heel, and the stick from the swamp." Any comments?

- *That shoe gets around.*

• Are we going to test it before or after we wash it?

• Let's wash one shoe, and test the other for germs.

• Is Justin really going to lick the brown Jell-O?

That was a good idea to wash one shoe, and test the other for germs. It will be an interesting comparison. Justin doesn't have to lick the solid media. We can gently touch his tongue with a sterile toothpick, then rub the toothpick on the medium. That should transfer germs to the medium. In fact, for all of our tests, we only need to touch the object to the medium to transfer microorganisms. I might need my shoes before the microorganisms have time to grow into a visible colony. Let's think about experimental consistency. As long as we make all of the plates the same way it should be okay. What controls should we use in this experiment?

• We could leave out the germy thing like we left out the dirty thing.

Great idea. We can leave one of the jars sealed, and not touch the medium at all.

• How will we know if the germs really came from my tongue? They might have been on the toothpick to start with.

Well, we could touch a fresh sterile toothpick to one jar of medium, then touch your tongue with another sterile toothpick and touch that toothpick to a second jar. We can see which jar grows more colonies. That would test if we really sterilized the toothpicks. Can anyone suggest a positive control? What could we put on the plates that we know will form colonies?

• A positive control would be putting germs on the medium. Where can we get some germs?

• Someone could cough on the medium.

• If that person wasn't sick, there might not be germs in the cough.

We can try coughing on the media. We can also try growing yeast—you know the kind people use when they bake bread? This kind of yeast won't make us sick, but yeast are microorganisms, and we should be able to grow them on our media. Let's write down a model.

MODEL: Less dirt will be found on the coin than on the pebble, stick, or shoe heel because the money is kept in a wallet or pocket, and not put on the ground. Germs will be found on the coin, tongue, fingers, stick, and shoe because none of these objects have been sterilized.

Recipe for Solid Medium[2] (makes about 24 jars)

2½ tablespoons molasses

1 cup water

3 tablespoons of laundry starch

8 envelopes unflavored gelatin

1 teaspoon Epsom salts

1 tablespoon baking powder

2 cups boiling water

24 pre-sterilized ½-pint canning jars with self-sealing lids

Mix molasses, water, and laundry starch in a large saucepan. Sprinkle unflavored gelatin over the mixture, and let stand one minute. Measure Epsom salts and baking powder into a very large mixing bowl. Pour a small amount of the boiling water onto the powders. Stir until foaming stops. Gradually add the rest of the water in small amounts, stirring to reduce foaming. When foaming has subsided, add water mixture to gelatin. Heat mixture to boiling. Simmer five minutes, stirring constantly.

Pour into pre-sterilized canning jars to a depth of about ½ inch, and cover immediately with self-sealing lids. The mixture solidifies more rapidly in the refrigerator. Do not inoculate medium until it has hardened. Use medium within a day or two of preparation. Do not open the sealed jars until you are ready to do the experiment. (A white precipitate in the bottoms of the jars does not affect the outcome of the experiment.)

After the medium has been inoculated, incubate the jars at 68–75°F. Molds and bacteria grow very slowly at cooler temperatures. The medium may melt at warmer temperatures.

How to Sterilize Canning Jars, Toothpicks, and Forceps

Wash canning jars and lids. Put lids in a pan of water and heat to 180°F. Do not boil self-sealing lids. The glass jars may break if they come in direct contact with the heat source, so place metal racks in the bottoms of two or three large cooking pots. Fill the cooking pots with water, and submerge the jars in the water. Boil for 10 minutes. Use tongs that have been heated in the boiling water for a few minutes to empty the jars and remove them from the boiling water. Pour medium into jars, and immediately cover jars with the self-sealing lids.

Sterile toothpicks are needed to inoculate the solid medium. The forceps are used for removing small objects from the surface of the medium after inoculation. Toothpicks and small forceps can be sterilized by placing them in boiling water for two or three minutes. Remove objects from boiling water with pre-boiled tongs or by pouring the hot water through a pre-sterilized metal strainer. Place sterilized toothpicks and forceps in empty sterile canning jars, and cover with a sterile lid. Objects left in contact with the air do not remain sterile.

Working with Microorganisms

Avoiding accidental contamination of sterile media is difficult so care must be taken in its preparation. I did not suggest using pressure cookers, or traditional food canning methods of sterilization because I wanted this experimental protocol to be as simple as possible. Contamination may occur, but chances are the experiment will not be ruined. Negative controls are essential because they demonstrate whether the microbial growth observed on the plates was caused by the experimental treatment, or was due to contamination of the medium by air-borne molds or bacteria. I used three negative controls in this experiment. Two jars were not exposed to any known germ-containing objects. One was left sealed, and the other was opened briefly. The third negative control was prepared by rubbing a sterile toothpick on the top of the medium. This tests the sterility of the toothpicks. Touching the medium with the germ-containing objects often leaves a mark in the surface of the gelatin. If microorganisms grow only on the mark, one can assume these microbes originated on the object that touched the medium. Mold colonies that occur on other locations of the plate were probably caused by airborne contaminants. Remember, nothing is sterile unless you have sterilized it in boiling water.

The exact type of microorganisms growing on the plates is not known, so children should *not* be allowed to touch colonies. When the experiment is over, tightly seal the jars, wrap them in a plastic bag, and dispose of them. If you really want to reuse the jars, loosen the lids, and put them in boiling water for five minutes. The tops of the jars need not be underwater. When the jars are cool enough to handle safely, pour the melted media into a large container like a plastic milk jug, seal it, and dispose of the container. The jars must be washed thoroughly before they can be used for another purpose. In my experience, cleaning up moldy canning jars is more trouble than it is worth.

Results

The results are given in Tables 7.1 and 7.2. The presentation of these results would be greatly enhanced with photographs of the coffee filters and jars.

Table 7.1. Appearance of Coffee Filters after Filtering Wash Water

TREATMENT	APPEARANCE OF FILTERS
Soapy water	Clean
Coin	About 10 tiny specs of dirt
Pebble	Fine layer of dirt
Stick	Medium-thick layer of dirt, plus some pieces of wood
Shoe heel	Fine layer of dirt
Dirt clod	Very thick layer of dirt; coffee filter not visible through dirt

Table 7.2. Appearance of Solid Media Three Days after Inoculation

TREATMENT	APPEARANCE OF SOLID MEDIA
Sealed jar	No microorganisms are observed on the plate.
Jar opened briefly	One small tan colony is growing near the edge.
Coin	Six tiny colonies are growing on the mark from the coin.
Sterile toothpick	White mold is growing around rim of jar, but no colonies are growing on scratch marks from toothpick.
Sterile toothpick rubbed on tongue	White colonies growing on scratch marks from toothpick.
Fingers	One colony of white mold is growing near one of the depressions in the media.
Shoe	Ten colonies of white mold are growing near dent from shoe heel.
Stick	White mold is growing on all four spots where the stick touched.
Cough	Two small white colonies of white mold are growing on the media.
Yeast[a]	Tan yeast are growing only along scratch marks from the toothpick.

a. Yeast were sprinkled on warm sugar water. After the yeast mixture started to foam, a toothpick was dipped in the mixture and used to inoculate the media.

Summary of results

1. The coin is not as dirty as the pebble, stick, or shoe.
2. There are germs on coins, fingers, shoes, sticks, and tongues.
3. No microorganisms could be cultured from fresh sterile toothpicks.
4. There are germs in the air.

Conclusions

1. Money is not the dirtiest stuff around. There is more dirt on pebbles, sticks, and shoes.
2. Money has germs on it.
3. The dirt on the coffee filters demonstrates how much visible grime is on the objects used in the experiment. The growth of microorganisms on the plates demonstrates whether the objects used in the experiment contain germs.
4. We cannot see a germ, but germs are on lots of things.
5. Germs are in the air. Simply opening the sterile jars allowed airborne molds to settle on the media and grow into colonies.
6. The colonies growing on the media that was coughed upon could have resulted from the cough or from contamination by airborne molds.
7. Putting money in your mouth is not a good idea.

A flow chart of this experiment is shown in Figure 7.1.

The imaginary children who planned this experiment clearly had previous experience with the brains-on method of scientific problem solving. I chose to invent scientifically savvy children so that this brainstorming session could be written as briefly as possible. In "real life," parents and teachers may have to provide more hints, leading questions, and explanations before children will comprehend experimental consistency and scientific controls. Neither concept is intuitive, but both are essential to the brains-on method.

People expect that actions have consequences. The ability to logically prove that observed consequences are the direct result of specific actions is the key to effective problem solving. By learning to design controlled experiments that test one parameter at a time, children acquire the skills to demonstrate cause and effect relationships, and thus gain a thorough understanding of the scientific method.

How does the remote control on the TV work?

My first reaction to this question was "When the battery is new, it works very well." Research was in order.[3]

The remote control is not connected to the TV with wires, so how does pressing a button on the remote change something on the TV? Pressing a button on the channel changer causes it to emit a signal in the form of pulses of light. Each

Is Money the Dirtiest Object Around?

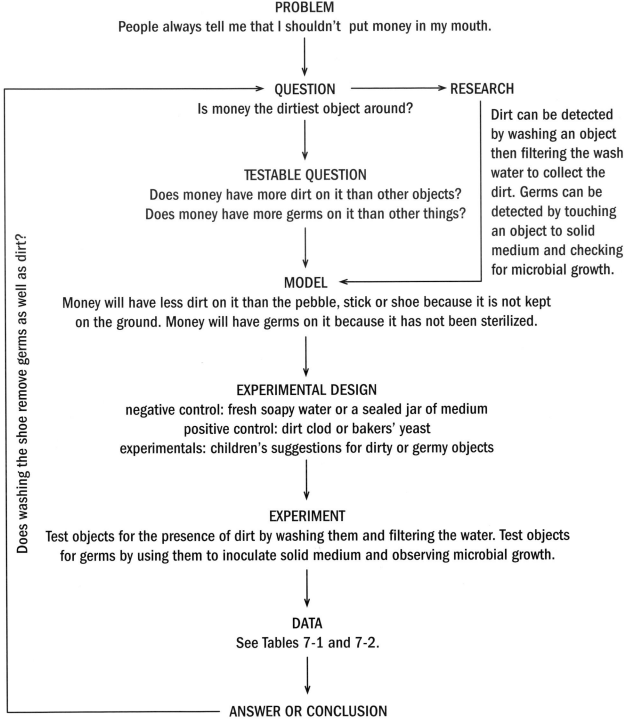

PROBLEM
People always tell me that I shouldn't put money in my mouth.

QUESTION ──────────→ **RESEARCH**
Is money the dirtiest object around?

Dirt can be detected by washing an object then filtering the wash water to collect the dirt. Germs can be detected by touching an object to solid medium and checking for microbial growth.

TESTABLE QUESTION
Does money have more dirt on it than other objects?
Does money have more germs on it than other things?

MODEL
Money will have less dirt on it than the pebble, stick or shoe because it is not kept on the ground. Money will have germs on it because it has not been sterilized.

EXPERIMENTAL DESIGN
negative control: fresh soapy water or a sealed jar of medium
positive control: dirt clod or bakers' yeast
experimentals: children's suggestions for dirty or germy objects

EXPERIMENT
Test objects for the presence of dirt by washing them and filtering the water. Test objects for germs by using them to inoculate solid medium and observing microbial growth.

DATA
See Tables 7-1 and 7-2.

ANSWER OR CONCLUSION
The coin is not as dirty as the pebble, stick, or shoe.
There are germs on coins, fingers, shoes, sticks, and tongues.

Does washing the shoe remove germs as well as dirt?

Figure 7.1. Flow Chart of the Dirt and Germ Experiment.

button has its own signal or code. A sensor on the TV detects the pulses of light and translates their code into electrical signals that change the channel or adjust the volume. The process is really just a modern-day version of "One, if by land, and two, if by sea . . ."[4] in that the remote control sends a coded message using light. We cannot see the beam because it is a special kind of light called "infrared" or IR light. The wavelengths of infrared light are longer than the range of wavelengths that the human eye can detect. Think of a rainbow or spectrum. The colors change from violet to red as the wavelengths of visible light lengthen. Infrared light is just beyond the red part of the spectrum, or "somewhere over the rainbow."[5]

Whenever doing experiments with electricity or electronics, I err on the side of caution and do the positive control first. Aim the remote at the TV, press a button, and observe the response. Did it do what it was supposed to do? The remote control and the television must be working properly in order to do the rest of the experiment.

In this experiment, the negative control also serves as a demonstration. Visible light is a good "non-infrared" control because the TV sensor cannot "see" visible light any more than our eyes can see infrared light. If the sensor on the TV could detect visible light, sunlight and electric lamps might interfere with the remote signal. The flashlight also sends a constant beam, not coded light pulses. Using visible light as the negative control lets the experimenters observe where the light goes. Turn on a regular flashlight and aim it at the television. The television should not respond, but the beam of light will be visible in a darkened room. Repeat the test with the remote control, holding the remote in the same position as the flashlight. Even though the infrared beam cannot be seen, the flashlight beam illuminates its path.

Does the infrared beam from the remote control behave like the visible light from the flashlight beam? The following questions might have resulted from a brainstorming session with children.

- A book can block the flashlight beam. Can a book block the light from the remote control?
- The light from a flashlight can pass through a clear plastic or glass. Will the light from remote control pass through glass or clear plastic?

- Does the beam from the remote have to hit the TV in order to work? How far away can it be? (The infrared sensor is usually on the front of the television or VCR.)
- Can the light from the flashlight or remote control be reflected off a mirror and onto the TV?

MODEL: The infrared light from the remote control will behave much like the visible light from a flashlight beam.

Table 7.3. Experiments with Visible and Infrared Light

TREATMENT	DETECTION OF VISIBLE LIGHT (FLASHLIGHT)	DETECTION OF INFRARED LIGHT (REMOTE)
Aimed at TV	Light on TV	TV turned on
	TV did not turn on	
Blocked with a book	Light on book	TV did not turn on
Passed through clear plastic	Light on TV	TV turned on
Aimed at ceiling	Light on ceiling	TV turned on
Aimed at floor	Light on floor	TV turned on
Aimed at wall facing TV	Light on wall	TV turned on
Aimed out window	Light on curtain	TV did not turn on
Aimed toward window, at mirror angled toward TV	Light on TV	TV turned on

Visible light was detected by observing a bright circle of light from a flashlight in a darkened room. Infrared light was detected by observing whether the television could be turned on with the remote control.

It was difficult to find a position in the room where the remote control did not turn on the television. Similarly, in a very dark room, shining the flashlight in most directions provided enough light to see the TV. The flashlight beam demonstrated how visible and infrared light beams reflect off walls, floors, and ceilings to reach the television.

The positions where the remote did and did not activate the television are diagramed in Figure 7.2. Placing a paper tube around the remote control focused the infrared beam. When the paper tube was in place, the remote control had to be aimed much closer to the TV in order to turn it on.

Conclusions

1. The infrared beam from the remote control acts much like visible light.
2. The infrared beam reflects off walls, ceilings, and even carpeted floors, and hits the sensor on the TV.
3. The TV was not turned on when the remote was pointed at the window because infrared light passes through glass, and is not reflected back toward the TV.
4. If a mirror was placed between the remote control and the window, the infrared beam was reflected back to the TV.

A flow chart of the remote control experiment is shown in Figure 7.3.

At the onset of this experiment, I knew next to nothing about TV channel changers; and until my curiosity was stimulated by a kindergartner's question, I had never actually thought about them. The scientific method is a way of learning about the world. In this experiment, the scientific method allowed me to go from total ignorance about a subject to interest, knowledge, and understanding. When children see adults learn from science, they gain a higher appreciation of both the adults and

Figure 7.2. Positions for the Remote Control.

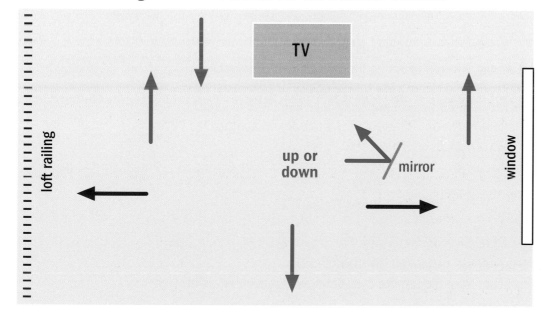

Green arrows indicate positions of the remote control that turned on the TV.
Red arrows indicate positions of the remote control that did *not* turn on the TV.

How Does the Remote Control on the TV Work?

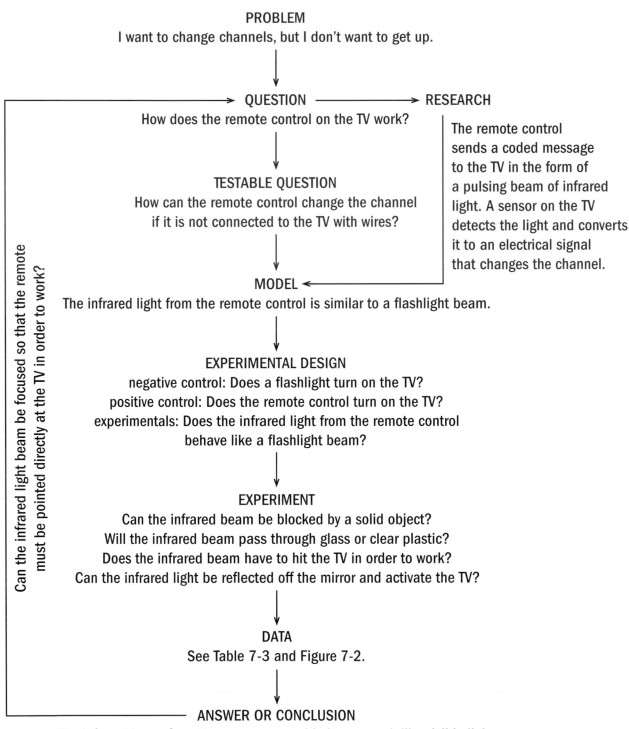

PROBLEM
I want to change channels, but I don't want to get up.

QUESTION ———→ **RESEARCH**
How does the remote control on the TV work?

The remote control sends a coded message to the TV in the form of a pulsing beam of infrared light. A sensor on the TV detects the light and converts it to an electrical signal that changes the channel.

TESTABLE QUESTION
How can the remote control change the channel if it is not connected to the TV with wires?

MODEL ←
The infrared light from the remote control is similar to a flashlight beam.

EXPERIMENTAL DESIGN
negative control: Does a flashlight turn on the TV?
positive control: Does the remote control turn on the TV?
experimentals: Does the infrared light from the remote control behave like a flashlight beam?

EXPERIMENT
Can the infrared beam be blocked by a solid object?
Will the infrared beam pass through glass or clear plastic?
Does the infrared beam have to hit the TV in order to work?
Can the infrared light be reflected off the mirror and activate the TV?

DATA
See Table 7-3 and Figure 7-2.

ANSWER OR CONCLUSION
The infrared beam from the remote control behaves much like visible light.

Can the infrared light beam be focused so that the remote must be pointed directly at the TV in order to work?

Figure 7.3. Flow Chart of the Remote Control Experiment.

science. No one has all the answers, but the brains-on method allows children and adults to become partners in investigation.

The concept of invisible light is somewhat puzzling. This experiment demonstrates that the mysterious infrared light emitted by a remote control behaves much like the light from a common flashlight. Because "seeing is believing," a flashlight was used to mark the location of the invisible infrared light signals. Confirming that both visible and infrared light can pass through glass, be blocked by solid objects, or be reflected off mirrors removes some of the magic from television channel changers.

The first two experiments in this chapter touch on a fundamental challenge of science. How do scientists detect, observe, and measure organisms, objects, or phenomena that cannot be seen? Sight is a predominant sense for humans, yet much of science is not visible to the human eye. In the germ experiment, a single bacterial or mold cell cannot be seen with the naked eye, so the microorganisms were allowed to multiply and form colonies consisting of billions of cells. These colonies were large enough to see. In the remote control experiment, a flashlight beam was used to approximate the location of an infrared light beam. Both experiments used a relatively simple technique to clarify an otherwise mysterious problem.

Why is apple cider brown?

I was given the opportunity to do a science experiment with my older son's first grade class. I was allotted two one-hour time periods to help the children plan and perform the experiment. Unfortunately, there was not time for the children to research the subject themselves, and I had to "lecture" them a bit. My main concern was to engage the children in a productive brainstorming session, but I first provided some background information on cells and enzymes. I was not overly concerned that they absorb all of this information, but I wanted to establish the rationale for doing the experiment the way we did it. The following is a transcript of my interaction with the children.

Does anyone know how apple cider is made? Has anyone visited a cider mill?

- *They squish up apples.*
- *They get the juice.*

- *They put it in jugs.*
- *I went to an apple juice factory once.*

The squishing is very important for our experiment. Has anyone noticed what happens to an apple core when you're done eating it?

- *It turns brown and mushy.*

I held up an apple that had been previously cut and "squished" by scoring it with the tines of a fork. What happens when we cut through the skin of an apple? What comes in contact with the inside of the apple once the skin is cut?

- *Air.*

So, we could form a hypothesis that air makes the apple turn brown. Scientists like to write equations. Scientific equations are sort of like sentences, and sort of like math problems. We could write:

$$\text{light apple} + \text{air} \rightarrow \text{brown apple}$$

There is a little more to it though. Remember when we talked about squishing the apple? If the apple isn't squished a little, it won't turn brown. We need to talk about two things: *cells* and *enzymes*. All living things are made up of cells. Cells are very tiny compartments. They are too small to be seen with your eye, but you can see them with a microscope. Have you ever seen a picture of a scientist looking through a microscope? Often, the scientist is looking at cells. Cells are like little houses with rooms. Different rooms do different things. Some contain the DNA, some get rid of wastes, some make energy, some do special jobs for special cells. The houses and rooms have walls. Water can go through the walls, but most other things require a special door and password to get into the house or room. A major function of the little rooms is to keep things separate.

Now let's talk about enzymes. Enzyme is a funny word. An enzyme is something that makes a reaction happen faster. Here is an example. Let's say there were toys all over the floor of your room. Probably you would pick them up eventually, before you had grown up. If your mom comes in and says that you can't go to your friend's house until your room is clean, you'd probably clean it up right away. In this case, your mom is like the enzyme. She gets the job done faster. In our apple experiment there is an enzyme that gets the job done faster.

$$\text{light apple} + \text{air} + \text{enzyme} \rightarrow \text{brown apple}$$

In an uncut apple, the air is kept out by the skin, and the enzyme is kept in a different room from the stuff that turns brown. When the apple is squished, the walls of the house and its rooms are broken, sort of like a wrecking ball hitting a building. That lets air and the enzyme come in contact with the stuff that turns brown. When the apple gets squished, everything gets mixed together.

$$\text{light apple (squished)} + \text{air} + \text{enzyme} \rightarrow \text{brown apple}$$

So in order for an apple to turn brown we need three things. Can anyone tell me what they are?

- *Air.*
- *A squished apple.*
- *That enzyme thing.*

When apple cider is made, there are all those things. Let's suppose we wanted to keep the apple from turning brown. What could we do?

- *Don't cut it.*
- *Don't squish it.*
- *Keep air away from it.*

Can anyone think of a way to keep air away from the apple? Can anyone think of anything we could put the apple in or something we could put on the apple to keep air away?[6]

I did not judge any of the suggestions. I mentioned that there was no refrigerator in the classroom, so we could not easily do that experiment. I also told the class that while putting an apple in outer space would work, we could not test that hypothesis in a classroom setting. The remaining suggestions were tested the following day.

- *Jordan: Put apple in the refrigerator.*
- *Becky: Put apple near the moon (outer space).*
- *Shane: Put apple in a plastic bag without any air.*
- *Patrick: Put apple in tin foil.*
- *Erin: Put apple in rolling paper (toilet paper).*
- *Gwen: Put apple in a box.*
- *Patrick, Jordan, Dustin: Coat apple with caramel.*
- *Anthony: Put apple in water.*
- *Lucas, Becky: Put apple in dirt or sand.*
- *Sam: Coat apple with white glue.*
- *Corey: Put apple in oil.*

Tomorrow we'll test your ideas. I'll come back tomorrow morning with lots of apples and all of the stuff you've suggested, and we'll try it. We'll see which treatments keep the apples from turning brown.

We are going to see a lot of apple slices that are various shades of brown, tan, or cream. How can we test how well our treatments worked? Can we tell if our treatments are better than doing nothing? How do we know if putting an apple slice in water, for example, makes it less brown than just leaving it out in the air?

The concept of negative controls is not intuitive. I could not get any child to suggest including an apple slice that had not been treated, and I had to tell them.

How are we going to know how light the apple was to begin with?

* *We could cut up an apple just before we look at the other slices.*

These are called controls. They are one of the most important parts of the experiment. If you don't know your starting point and your ending point, it is difficult to judge how well your treatments worked.

While the children did not grasp the importance of controls in this introductory discussion, they did seem to understand the concept when we did the experiment. When we analyzed the results, each treated apple slice was compared to a freshly cut apple slice and to an untreated apple slice that had been cut and scored at the same time as the experimental slice. When the children were asked to rank the treated apple slices in comparison to the controls, they could see the need for experimental boundaries.

This experiment was designed to determine methods to *prevent* apple browning, so the positive control, or the treatment that was assured to work well, was the freshly cut apple slice. We knew from previous experience that in an uncut apple, the skin prevents air from coming in contact with the chemical that turns brown. A freshly cut apple was the lightest possible apple slice, so that was chosen to be the positive control. The negative control, or the conditions that were assured to yield the darkest possible apple slice, was the cut, scored, but untreated slice. Previous experience had shown that this yielded dark brown stripes on the apple slices. The no-treatment negative control was expected to produce the darkest apple slices and the bottom boundary for the data.

The apples used in the experiment were red delicious. I had previously tested several varieties of apples for the speed and extent of the browning reaction. Red delicious and Macintosh apples worked well in this experiment, but tart green apples such as Granny Smith browned very little. Apples purchased at farm stands or farmers' markets tend to turn brown faster than apples from the supermarket. The most important factor in apple browning is squishing the apple. Simply cutting the apple does not result in much browning. I scored each apple slice with a fork to ensure that many cells would be broken, and the enzyme would come in contact with the chemical that turns brown. This is an extra control because dark brown lines form where the apple cells have been broken. These brown lines can be compared to the lighter surface of the apple slice.

On the second day, I brought the treatments, apples, and accessories to the classroom. Each child who had suggested a treatment was designated as leader of a group of two or three. The class sat in a circle on the floor, and each team sat together. We did the treatments one at a time. The team leader performed the treatment (putting glue on the apple, wrapping it in foil, etc.) For each group, I cut and scored two apple slices. One slice was given to the children to be treated, while the other served as a negative control. The apple slices were cut and scored immediately before treatment. All of the apple slices were placed on previously labeled plastic trays in order to keep track of the treatments. By the time the ninth treatment had been done, the first apple slices had turned brown. The class evaluated the treatments in the order they were done. Each experimental slice was compared to its negative (no treatment) and positive (freshly cut) controls. Apples treated with dirt, caramel, and glue were washed before their color was assessed.

> **MODEL:** Glue and caramel will work best to keep air away from apple slices because air diffuses slowly through these thick substances. The plastic bag should prevent apple browning if all the air inside the bag can be pushed out.

We concluded that thick, sticky substances like glue and caramel worked best at keeping the air away from the apple. Water, oil, and aluminum foil were partially effective. I was surprised to see how well toilet paper worked. That apple slice was thoroughly wrapped, almost mummified. Figure 7.4 is a diagram of the apple browning experiment.

Aside from the caramel and water treatments, the results of this experiment have few practical applications. What did the children learn from this scientific experience? The children were introduced to the biological concepts of cells and enzymes,

Table 7.4. Which Treatments Prevent Apple Browning?

CHILD	TREATMENT	COLOR OF CUT, SCORED, BUT UNTREATED APPLE (NEGATIVE CONTROL)	COLOR OF EXPERIMENTAL APPLE	COLOR OF FRESHLY CUT APPLE (POSITIVE CONTROL)
Jordan	plastic bag	dark	darker[a]	light
Patrick	aluminum foil	dark	medium to dark	light
Erin	toilet paper	dark	medium	light
Gwen	box	dark	dark	light
Dustin	caramel	dark	light	light
Anthony	water	dark	medium to dark[b]	light
Lucas	dirt	medium[c]	medium	light
Sam	white glue	dark	light	light
Corey	oil	dark	medium	light

a. The apple in the plastic bag was darker than the untreated apple. Jordon worked very hard to push all of the air out of the plastic bag. He probably pushed so hard on the apple slice that he broke additional cells, so the experimental slice was more "squished" than its negative control.

b. The score marks from the fork were light at one end of the apple slice and dark at the other.

c. This untreated apple did not turn very dark in comparison to the other untreated slices. An unexplained glitch such as this one demonstrates the value of having a negative control for each apple slice.

and they started to experiment with the physical properties of gasses. Most importantly, they discovered that they could create their own science. The brainstorming format reinforced the idea that the children's ideas have value. The students were given an opportunity to apply previously acquired knowledge to a current problem. The students learned that the results of an experiment are not always known before the experiment starts. The children were introduced to the concept of controls, enabling them to analytically examine cause and effect relationships. When they evaluated the treatments, they were required to judge the effectiveness of their ideas, and draw conclusions from their data. Spreading white glue on an apple slice may appear foolish to the casual observer, but this idea demonstrates a fundamental understanding of both biology and physics. These young experimenters are clearly developing analytical problem solving skills.

Why Is Apple Cider Brown?

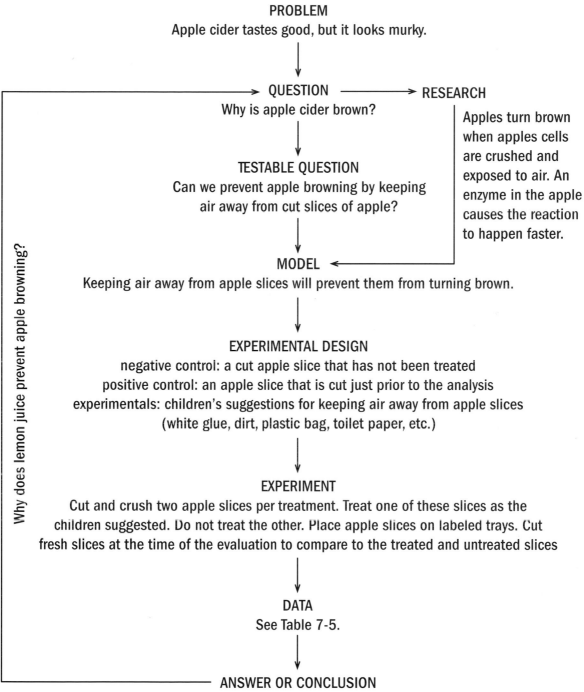

PROBLEM
Apple cider tastes good, but it looks murky.

QUESTION → **RESEARCH**
Why is apple cider brown?

Apples turn brown when apples cells are crushed and exposed to air. An enzyme in the apple causes the reaction to happen faster.

TESTABLE QUESTION
Can we prevent apple browning by keeping air away from cut slices of apple?

MODEL
Keeping air away from apple slices will prevent them from turning brown.

EXPERIMENTAL DESIGN
negative control: a cut apple slice that has not been treated
positive control: an apple slice that is cut just prior to the analysis
experimentals: children's suggestions for keeping air away from apple slices
(white glue, dirt, plastic bag, toilet paper, etc.)

EXPERIMENT
Cut and crush two apple slices per treatment. Treat one of these slices as the children suggested. Do not treat the other. Place apple slices on labeled trays. Cut fresh slices at the time of the evaluation to compare to the treated and untreated slices

DATA
See Table 7-5.

ANSWER OR CONCLUSION
Thick substances like glue and caramel prevent browning by limiting the diffusion of air to the apple slice.

Why does lemon juice prevent apple browning?

Figure 7.4. Flow Chart of the Apple Browning Experiment.

How do you make a parachute for a Beanie Baby?

After doing some research,[7] several family members designed and built parachutes. The designs are shown in Figure 7.5. "Zed" was constructed from the bottoms of two brown paper shopping bags. The edges of the bag were folded over and stiffened with masking tape, and six pieces of kite string suspended a rubber band from the paper bag. The rubber band held the passenger. "White" consisted of a 20-inch square of butcher paper stiffened with plastic strips cut from gallon milk containers. Four pieces of kite strings connected the corners of the paper to a rubber band passenger restraint. "Navy" and "Cooca" are similar to one another in design. "Navy" was made by attaching a paper plate to an 8-ounce paper cup with two pieces of yarn. The passenger rode in the paper cup. "Cooca" was made from a disposable plastic plate attached to a 4-ounce paper cup with four strings. "The Ram" was a 7½ × 6-inch oval paper sail. The passenger was inserted into a paper ring taped to the sail.

Table 7.5. Falling Times (in seconds) for the Beanie Baby Parachutes

PARACHUTE	TRIAL 1	TRIAL 2	TRIAL 3	TRIAL 4	TRIAL 5	TRIAL 6
no parachute (negative control)	0.70	0.71	0.80	0.64	0.81	0.79
"Navy"	0.93	0.78[a]	1.05	1.36	0.99	1.14
"Cooca"	1.15	1.14	1.20	1.27	1.13	1.09
"White"	2.15	1.95	2.16	1.36[b]	1.87	1.93
"The Ram"	0.85	0.83	0.83	0.89	0.90	0.96
"Zed"	1.69	1.80	1.70	1.72	1.39	1.56
"Zed" with no rider[c]	1.66	1.71	1.80	1.61	1.65	1.71
"Zed" with two "Speedys"	1.41	1.30	1.40	1.59	1.46	1.46

a. Speedy fell out.   b. Parachute collapsed.   c. Parachute flipped over in all trials.

MODEL: The larger parachutes ("Zed" and "White") will be the slowest because they provide the most air resistance.

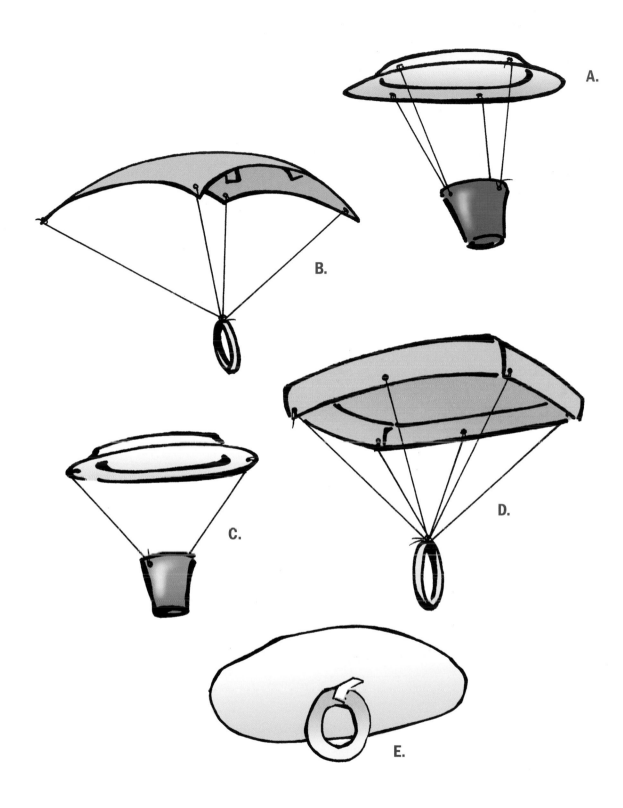

Figure 7.5. Parachute Designs. A is "Cooca," B is "White," C is "Navy,"
D is "Zed," and E is "The Ram."

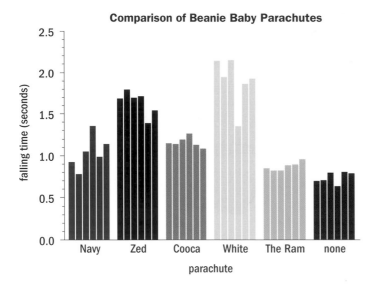

Comparison of Beanie Baby Parachutes

Figure 7.6. Comparison of Beanie Baby Parachutes. All of the parachutes except "The Ram" reduced the falling speed of the Teeny Beanie. "White" and "Zed" often fell the slowest, but not in every instance. The passenger falling from the parachute caused the low point in "Navy's" times (second bar). The low point in "White's" times (fourth bar) occurred when the parachute collapsed.

Figure 7.7. An Extra Passenger Does Not Affect "Zed's" Falling Time. The falling speed of "Zed" was similar with no, one, or two passengers. The parachute inverted in all runs without a passenger.

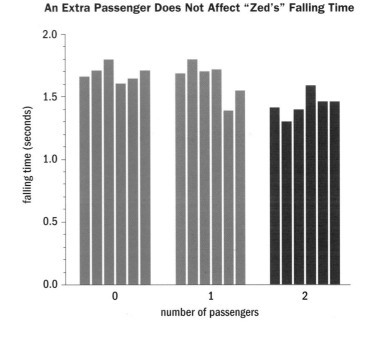

An Extra Passenger Does Not Affect "Zed's" Falling Time

Every parachute was tested in six separate trials by dropping it and its rider over the railing of a loft. A stopwatch was used to measure the time (in seconds) required for the parachute and rider to reach the floor below, a distance of 145 inches (398.3 cm). The same passenger, a Teeny Beanie turtle named "Speedy," was used in all runs. The negative control was omitting the parachute. The "Zed" parachute was also tested without a rider and with two "Speedys." The data are shown in Table 7.6 and Figures 7.6 and 7.7. Any trial in which the parachute hit a wall was disqualified and repeated.

Conclusions

1. All of the parachutes except "The Ram" increase the falling time of a Teeny Beanie. Falling times with "The Ram" parachute are similar to the no-parachute control.

2. Except in the fourth trial, "White" provides the slowest runs. The fourth trial could be discounted as a glitch because the parachute collapsed, and "White" could be declared the winner. (One hopes that professional parachute manufacturers do not adopt this attitude.) When all of the data is considered, however, the falling times for "White," "Zed," "Navy," and "Cooca" overlap.

3. The important considerations in parachute constructions seem to be size of the sail (bigger sails provide more air resistance and fall more slowly), and the stability of the parachute (floppy parachutes tend to collapse during flight).

4. The heaviest parachute (Zed) did not fall the fastest.

5. "Zed" falls at the same speed when riderless or with one rider. Adding a second passenger tends to increase falling speed, although the falling times with one and two passengers overlap.

6. Almost any parachute (except "The Ram") is better than no parachute. The design flaws of "The Ram" are its small size and great flexibility. The sail is not large or stiff enough to provide adequate air resistance.

Figure 7.8 is a flow chart for the parachute experiment.

In doing the parachute experiment, children developed skills in measurement and data acquisition. Several of the runs were completed in less than a second reinforcing the importance of using care and consistency in performing experiments. The numerical results provide practice in graphing and data analysis. The experimenters needed to examine the results carefully in order to decide if any of the parachutes could be considered the "safest."

The brains-on approach helps children learn how to solve problems. Children discover that information can be obtained about nearly any subject through experimentation and library research. Brainstorming helps children clarify their questions, and plan experiments. Experimentation encourages systematic methods, quantitation, and measurement skills. Data analysis teaches graphing and numerical skills, and encourages honesty. Collaborative interactions with adults show children how to accept responsibility, appreciate their own capabilities, and trust and understand their teachers. The brains-on method presents a "can-do" philosophy. Children are

How Do You Make a Parachute for a Beanie Baby?

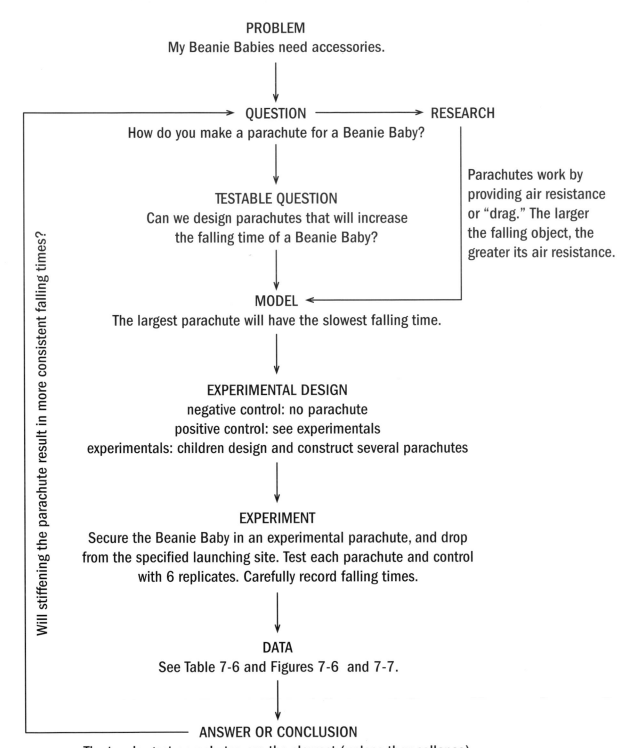

PROBLEM
My Beanie Babies need accessories.

QUESTION ──────────→ **RESEARCH**
How do you make a parachute for a Beanie Baby?

Parachutes work by providing air resistance or "drag." The larger the falling object, the greater its air resistance.

TESTABLE QUESTION
Can we design parachutes that will increase the falling time of a Beanie Baby?

MODEL
The largest parachute will have the slowest falling time.

EXPERIMENTAL DESIGN
negative control: no parachute
positive control: see experimentals
experimentals: children design and construct several parachutes

EXPERIMENT
Secure the Beanie Baby in an experimental parachute, and drop from the specified launching site. Test each parachute and control with 6 replicates. Carefully record falling times.

DATA
See Table 7-6 and Figures 7-6 and 7-7.

ANSWER OR CONCLUSION
The two largest parachutes are the slowest (unless they collapse).

Will stiffening the parachute result in more consistent falling times?

Figure 7.8. Flow Chart of the Parachute Experiment.

acknowledged for their inquisitiveness, creativity, and analytical skills. Children also learn that they can cooperate with their parents and teachers to discover the answers to their questions.

NOTES

1. Vicki Cobb, *Dirt and Grime Like You've Never Seen* (New York: Scholastic, 1998); Carrie Heeter (executive producer), Randy Russell (director/programmer), and Catherine McGowan (microbiologist), *Microbe Zoo*, CD-ROM *for Windows and Macintosh* (Peregrine Publishers in association with the Communication Technology Laboratory, the Center for Microbial Ecology, and the College of Education at Michigan State University, 1996).

2. Pre-made solid media is available from some commercial scientific supply companies.

3. David Macaulay, *The Way Things Work 2.0*, CD-ROM *for Windows and Macintosh* (New York: DK Multimedia, 1996).

4. Henry Wadsworth Longfellow, "Paul Revere's Ride," *Tales of a Wayside Inn* (Boston: Ticknor and Fields, 1863).

5. Harold Arlen (composer) and E. Y. (Yip) Harburg (lyricist), *Somewhere over the Rainbow*, © Warner Brothers, 1938.

6. Apple browning can also be prevented by inhibiting the enzyme. Lemon juice retards apple browning because the enzyme does not work efficiently in an acidic environment.

7. Jack Challoner, *Make It Work! / Flight* (New York: Scholastic, 1995).

Method for Younger Children

Suppose . . . we show to the child . . . the cocoon unfolding, the butterfly actually emerging. The knowledge, which comes from actual seeing, is worthwhile.

—Thomas A. Edison

CAN THE BRAINS-ON TECHNIQUE BE USED BY CHILDREN IN PRESCHOOL, kindergarten, and the lower elementary grades? In my opinion (and in my experience), the answer is yes. Younger children just require more help and patience from adults. The brains-on method is designed to foster cooperation between adults and children. As parents and teachers help children investigate their scientific interests, both the children and the adults will acquire new information. This democratic partnership between children and adults helps children develop independence, trust, learning skills, and teaching skills.

Questions

Younger children often pose wonderful questions. The four experiments discussed in Chapter 7 were developed from questions asked by three kindergartners and one first grader. Young children are curious, and frequently verbalize questions about phenomena that older children and adults take for granted. In the brains-on method, children are encouraged to develop their curiosity, express their ideas, and think logically. Young children benefit from this approach as much as older children. The role of the adults can be tailored to the maturity of the children.

When collecting questions from younger children, an adult must record the question. Few if any of the questions I collected from kindergartners and preschoolers were written in a child's handwriting. (Consequently, these questions were easy to decipher.) For designing experiments, the questions asked by young children may require some clarification and definition of terms. Refining questions in a brainstorming session is a useful academic exercise for children. (See Chapter 7: "Is money the dirtiest stuff around?" and Chapter 3: "Can orchids tell when you touch them?")

Brainstorming and Experimental Planning

From my experience, brainstorming works remarkably well with children in first grade. The brainstorming session described in Chapters 3 and 7 for the apple browning experiment was done by first graders near the beginning of the school year. This was my first "teaching experience" in a classroom setting, and my first attempt to brainstorm with a large group of children. I was pleasantly surprised. Brainstorming with children was easier than I expected.

Young children may require more adult guidance to achieve a good brainstorming session, but the results are gratifying. Parents and teachers may find that asking leading questions stimulates young children's creativity. Think about the concepts that you would like the brainstorming session to realize, and how the children could be encouraged to think of them. The children may suggest ideas of startling creativity.

Brainstorming sessions should be shorter for younger children. The brainstorming session for the sledding experiment (Chapter 3) is a dramatization, and written as a continuous dialog. Planning the experiment over several days could be more effective. The children's behavior will be a good indicator for determining the length of a brainstorming session.

Experimental consistency may be an odd concept to younger children. The use of examples can help them understand why it is important to vary only one thing between experimental trials. Even very young children will comprehend why one rider should do all of the timed sled runs, for example, when they realize that some of their classmates are more skilled at sledding than others. In some cases, the adult in charge of the experiment can assure experimental consistency, allowing the children to focus on the main concept of the experiment. Several apples of the same variety can be purchased for the apple browning experiment or cups of the same size can be obtained for the bean seedling experiment.

Hypothesis testing (proposing a model and testing it) is often inappropriate for very young children, but they learn much through observation. My seven-year-old son viewed the bean growth experiment as a competition between the three soils, and followed the progress of the plants as if they were participating in a sporting event. My four-year-old son, on the other hand, had little interest in the type of soil used in the experiment, but he enjoyed watching the formation of roots and shoots in the no-soil controls, and observing how rapidly the bean plants grew. Both boys learned from the experiment; they just learned different things.

Controls

Young children understand experimental controls in practice if not in theory. They comprehend demonstrations of cause and effect relationships, before they are prepared to design negative controls. When planning the apple browning experiment with a first grade class, none of my hints, suggestions, or leading questions inspired the children to suggest using a negative control. No one suggested comparing the experimental apple slices to apple slices that had been cut at the same time, but left untreated. When we did the experiment however, each treated apple slice was placed on a plastic tray between its positive (freshly cut) and negative (untreated) controls. The children could then see that we needed control samples for comparison.

Children who are not yet ready to propose a model and test it can benefit from simple hands-on science demonstrations. Every experiment and science demonstration should include negative controls to prove that the observed results were caused by the experimental treatment. Including negative controls validates experimental results and introduces the essence of the scientific method. My older son's first grade teacher demonstrated how blubber keeps sea mammals warm in arctic waters. She had each child place one hand in a plastic bag filled with vegetable shortening. The children then put both hands in a tub of ice water. The no-Crisco control hand felt much colder than its blubbery counterpart. The negative control emphasized the cause and effect relationship between the experimental treatment and the result.

Doing the Experiment

Crowd control is often an issue with the younger set. Science is exciting especially because experiments may be a deviation from classroom routine. One solution to this problem is to divide the "crowd" into smaller groups, and assign each group one task in the experiment. Each child then has more responsibility and a greater personal stake in the outcome of the experiment. The apple browning experiment was amenable to this approach because of the large number of experimental treatments. The class was divided into groups of two or three, and each group was responsible for doing one treatment. The experiment was done one treatment at a time, and the entire class watched each group perform its part of the experiment. A semblance of order was maintained, and each group had its moment in the spotlight.

Safety issues are a special concern with younger children, and care must be taken to choose experiments that can be performed safely. Adults should always monitor experiments involving electricity, sharp and pointed objects, intense heat, and hazardous chemicals. When working with young children, adults should perform potentially dangerous manipulations. Some experiments are simply more suitable for older children who have more experience in following directions, and greater manual dexterity.

Young children sometimes demonstrate an uncanny ability to produce potentially dangerous situations. I thought that the apple browning experiment was relatively hazard free, but I learned differently. I was surprised when a few of the boys in the class became excited and tried to grab the knife I had brought to slice the apples. Fortunately, my large pocketknife could be closed and hidden in my pocket when not in use. In this case, "out of sight, out of mind" worked for the duration of the experiment.

The best experiments for young children are straightforward and produce simple data. Parents and teachers may have to examine several questions that are suitable for experimentation before finding one that is appropriate for younger children. The Beanie Baby parachute experiment (Chapter 7) is manageable by first graders. They can construct and launch parachutes, and record the falling times accurately. First graders may not have heard of decimals, but they can certainly write the numerical equivalent of "one-point-one-five" in the correct spot in a simple table. An adult may need to handle the stopwatch because measuring very small time periods requires quick reaction times. If this experiment is done with preschoolers, the adults should be prepared to repair any parachutes that are damaged by rough handling.

Complex experiments require more adult intervention. I performed the germs-on-a-coin experiment (Chapter 7) with a preschooler, a kindergartner, a first grader, and a second grader. All four boys were interested in doing the experiment and observing the results. I prepared the sterile media, and closely monitored the inoculations. I also performed delicate manipulations like removing the coin from the surface of the solid media with sterile tweezers.

Keeping a Laboratory Notebook

Children who lack skill in writing need help with their laboratory notebooks. Assisting older children may ensure that they do not put aside their creative ideas to concentrate on the writing. Compiling a laboratory notebook requires a good deal of effort. This task can be shared with adults so the labor does not inhibit the children's enthusiasm for the project. The following suggestions may make the preparation of a notebook seem less daunting.

❶ Have an adult record brainstorming sessions. Even children who write well should not be bothered with recording ideas in the middle of a creative exchange. The children can condense the important concepts into notebook format later.

❷ Make a classroom notebook instead of individual notebooks. For experiments done by young children, an adult can be the scribe, and record the children's ideas and observations. Try to record the children's own words when possible. Children's spontaneous observations often make charming additions to a scientific poster.

❸ Divide and conquer the problem. One group of children can write the experimental methods, while another group records the data. This allows children to concentrate on a limited set of tasks, and each group of children "owns" a specific aspect of the experiment.

❹ Consider preparing a fill-in-the-blank worksheet to "jump start" children who are having trouble with the idea of a laboratory notebook. While I believe that a laboratory notebook should be a creative personal expression, sometimes a little extra help is needed. Written forms containing statements such as "The materials (things) we used in this experiment were _____" may be necessary for the first few experiments.

Prepare blank tables before doing the experiment. Provide plenty of space to record data and observations. The blank tables aid in data organization, and prevent samples from being forgotten. The tables can be prepared on a chalkboard or poster for use by the entire class, or photocopied on sheets of paper and taped into notebooks.

Analyzing the Data

The math ability of the experimenters must be considered when doing experiments with younger children. In some cases the quantitative aspects of an experiment can be de-emphasized. For example, presenting the data in bar graph format is preferable for children who have not learned Cartesian coordinates. Sometimes choosing experiments that yield non-numeric data is best for younger children.

Preschoolers or kindergartners could present the data from the bean seedling experiment (Chapters 4 and 6 and Appendix 2) without using numbers at all. Pressed and dried bean plants could be glued directly onto the poster, allowing the audience to see and judge the results for themselves. If first or second graders were doing the bean seedling experiment, they would not have to draw a graph as complicated as Figure 6.7 to see that bean plants do not grow well in sand. A simple bar graph like Figure 6.8 tells the same story. Older children could prepare a graph like Figure 6.7 as a group project with each child or research team responsible for measuring and plotting the growth of one plant. The data could be compiled at the end of the experiment.

The apple browning experiment (Chapters 3, 4, and 7) could be adapted for children who cannot yet read by recording the data in pictorial form. The data table could be made with pictures indicating the treatments (aluminum foil, white glue, water, etc.). Children could color pictures of apple slices pale yellow, tan, or brown to record their data.

The analysis of experimental data can also be used to stretch children's computational skills, because the scientific experience may motivate children to learn new mathematical concepts. If the students are interested in learning which sled is the fastest, and the answer can be found by graphing the data, then perhaps that is a good reason to learn how to construct and interpret a graph.

Preparing the Poster

Making a scientific poster can be a big job, but one that children will enjoy if the task does not become overwhelming. Do the lettering or typing for them if writing is a chore for the experimenters. The poster should be legible, and even the best efforts of young children may be nearly indecipherable. Use the children's own words on the poster, but help with the writing. Recording children's comments while the experiment is in progress will help connect the children with their experiment, and provide extra information for the poster. (Recording children's words is easier when small groups of children are doing an experiment, or if additional adults are present to help.) Young children can feel responsible for creating the poster by helping to paste pictures and text on the poster board, choosing photographs, and preparing the illustrations and graphs. Older children may wish to share the responsibilities of making a scientific poster. One group of children can write out the methods, while another writes the conclusions. In order for the children to feel like they "own" the poster, they should prepare as much of it as possible. Adults should help prevent the task from becoming a chore.

The Venus Flytrap Experiment

Our oldest son was assigned his first independent science project when he was in kindergarten. As both his father and I are Ph.D.-level scientists, we were confident that we could do a nifty kindergarten science experiment, but we wanted the project to belong to our son. A few weeks earlier, our son had asked, "How does a Venus flytrap catch flies?" so we decided to investigate that question.

The project was due on the second day after the winter holiday break. Our family had previously planned to spend the holiday in California so we did the experiment while we were on vacation. We purchased a Venus flytrap plant and a few crickets, caught some spiders and flies, and gathered up a notebook and a camera. We wrote down our son's own words about the experiment, and took photographs of him "feeding" the plant. We heeded our son's suggestions about the composition of the photographs, and included dinosaur toys and action figures with large teeth in the photos next to the spiky leafed plant. While our kindergartner did not propose a model of how he thought the plant caught insects, and formally test this hypothesis, he did learn several things from the experiment.

1. The hairs on the leaf must be touched twice in fairly rapid succession to make the leaf close. (This is how the plant "checks" to make certain that a living insect, not a wind-blown twig, has touched the leaf.)
2. When the leaf closes without a bug in it (negative control), it will reopen in one day. (Leaves can be made to close by touching the leaf hairs twice with a toothpick or tweezers.)
3. When the leaf traps an insect, it reopens after a week, and the "skeleton" (exoskeleton) of the insect can be seen on the surface of the leaf.

We helped our son prepare the poster. I wrote his words on poster board, and helped him glue on the photographs. We left the plant with a friend in California, and returned to Michigan.

For his poster presentation, our son wanted to have a real Venus flytrap to supplement the information on his poster. Michigan's climate in January is rarely temperate, and that year the temperature was hovering around 10°F. Venus flytraps are native to the bogs of North Carolina, and do not tolerate cold weather. My best efforts to shield that tender plant from the cold were unsuccessful. All the leaves were closed and withered by the time I got the plant to our son's classroom. Fortunately, sufficient information had been recorded on the poster because a live demonstration was impossible. Despite months of pampering on a warm windowsill, the Venus flytrap never recovered from the shock.

Problem Solving

The brains-on method is adaptable for people of all ages. While most of this book is directed at elementary school children, the methods can be modified for younger and older students. Adult scientists in professional research laboratories employ similar techniques. Children should be encouraged to develop problem-solving skills early in their education because these techniques make children more efficient learners throughout their education and their lives. Modern science is highly sophisticated, but the basics of experimental design and scientific problem solving are quite straightforward and appropriate for young children.

Children's Questions

THE FOLLOWING IS A LIST OF QUESTIONS I COLLECTED FROM ELEMENTARY school children. I prepared a flier requesting children's questions about science, and made it available to two schools in my neighborhood. Responding to the flier was a favor not an assignment, so not all the grades are equally represented. I have noted when a question was asked more than once by different students within the same grade level.

Preschool and Kindergarten

Why are snow and ice white?

Can mice climb?

Why do snails have slime?

Do water snakes die on land?

Why do crabs wave their claws?

How does a parachute fly without wings?

How long can a polar bear hold its breath?

How do you make chemicals?

Why can you get zapped by electricity?

Why do clouds move?

Why does the earth spin?

Why do we hiccup?

How do ants know where the first one goes when following each other?

Where is the mouth on an octopus?

What are deer antlers made of?

Are birds colorblind?

What is the most valuable gem?

Is money the dirtiest object around?

Why do we have thunder and lightning?

Why do snakes (or shrimp) shed their skin?

How does a train stay on the tracks?

How do people get inside the TV?

Where do ants go after they taste poison?

Why do different animals make different sounds?

What causes a bee to make a "buzz, buzz" sound?

What causes a bunny to hop?

Why is the sky blue? *(asked three times)*

Why does the sun follow us?

How does rain fall from the sky?

What is fog?

Why can't helium balloons float upside down?

Where do fireflies get their light?

Why do people have hair "there"?

Why do leaves change color?

Why do some trees lose their leaves and evergreens don't?

Why are spiders sometimes green?

What makes thunder boom?

Do butterflies have feet?

How do they make medicine out of plants?

How much air in a "floatie" would it take for an elephant to float?

Who goes down the slide faster, bigger or smaller kids?

How much oxygen can your lungs hold?

Why don't spiders stick to their own webs?

When the bathtub is draining, is that a tornado in the water?

What causes earthshakes (earthquakes)?

Why do flowers smell good?

Why do our hands and feet get wrinkled in the bathtub?

Does a caterpillar weigh more or less than a butterfly?

How do the stars shine so bright?

How long do ladybugs live?

How do skunks make their smell?

Where did the very first tree come from?

How do the seasons change? *(asked two times)*

How do they know space goes on to infinity?

What is the difference between insects and bugs?

Why is milk white?

IIow do fish eat?

Is a grasshopper a bug?

Why does an airplane slow down in the sky?

How does a microwave get hot?

Where does the thread for a spider's web come from?

How do flowers get their colors?

How many times has Mt. St. Helens exploded?

Are there real unicorns?

What are rhinos' horns made of?

Why does the earth turn?

How do tornadoes form?

Why do some animals hibernate?

Why does gravity make things drop?

How do light bulbs light?

How does the remote control on the TV work?

Are there really aliens in space?

First Grade

Why is 50°F cool and 50°C warm?

Why do the bodies of Colobus monkeys look like skunks?

Why is apple cider brown?

When the basketball is right inside the hoop, how does it bounce out if gravity
  pulls it down?

How does evolution work?

What is a scab?

How do crystals form?

How big can crystals get?

How does hair grow?

Is a pillow matter?

Is air matter?

Is paper matter?

Is my mom's sleepy foot matter?

What happens to the gas when it's put into the car?

What happens to food when it's put into the compost?

How did the ice turn into water?

Why did the steam rise in the air?

What if you put water in a balloon?

What temperature does snow change from ice to water?

What makes a solid turn into a gas?

What makes popcorn pop?

How do clouds change into air?

Why do helium balloons float?

Why is the world round?

Why does water turn to ice when it's cold?

Why does water bubble on the stove?

Why does water evaporate? *(asked four times)*

What is matter?

How does matter change state?

How does water change its shape?

What makes a cloud?

How can the gas go?

Do raisins get moldy?

Second Grade

How do people get different color skin?

How fast in miles per hour does water run from the faucet in the bathtub at its
    highest pressure?

How are sand dunes formed?

What animal jumps the highest in proportion to it's own size, and which gets highest off the earth?

Where did the meteorite hit the earth?

Did anybody make it to Pluto?

Why is the sky blue?

How were humans created?

Did apes evolve from monkeys?

Did a big bubble of gas really surround the earth before there was any life on earth?

How does medicine know where to go?

How do scientists name all the animals of the earth?

What is lava?

How much blood can a leach suck from a person?

How much have crocodiles and alligators changed since the dinosaur days?

Third Grade

Why does the light turn on so fast when we flip the light switch?

Can orchids tell when you touch them?

Can underwater animals hear you talking if you are not touching the water?

If there are atoms, and we cannot see them, how do we know they are there?

When you cut a paper with scissors, do you cut the molecules in half?

Fourth Grade

Why are some animals live born and some egg born?

Why are some rocks shiny and others dull?

Why do some animals like sun and some like the shade?

Why are rocks minerals?

Why does a roller coaster (or car ride) make me feel sick?

Why is a desert so hot?

What makes a king cobra not a true cobra?

What forms an atom?

What makes a mineral?

Why do sharks attack people?

How many eyes does a tarantula have?

Is lead a metal or a mineral?

Were house cats ever wild?

Why is a horse called a horse?

Why is science called science?

How many inches are in a mile?

How do rocks form? *(asked five times)*

What is the scientific name for Koala?

Why do mammals have hair?

What makes a mammal a mammal?

When were reptiles first born?

How big are all the planets put together?

How does a plant grow?

How is water made? *(asked two times)*

How is candy made?

How wide is the earth?

What is the scientific name for a bear?

How big is the world?

What is the most endangered species in the world?

Are all the animals going to die?

How did the world begin?

I want to know more about soccer and football.

When you play sports, what makes you sweat?

What is the meaning of life? *(asked two times)*

Are we going to die?

Is there going to be a city on the moon?

How does an animal survive in cold weather?

Why are some animals tame?

How did people make lead?

What is a butterfly's wing made of?

Why do you play soccer with your feet?

Where do my permanent teeth come from?

On what continent did most dinosaurs live?

Are we ever upside down on planet earth?

Why do butterflies need powder on their wings to fly?

How many worms do birds eat in a day?

Why does the human body need food to stay alive?

How does the brain know what to do and when to do it?

Who holds the record for the most goals in a half?

How can you put your finger through fire without burning it?

How do most animals communicate?

How long does it take most rock to form?

How hot is the sun?

How long around is the earth?

How many rings are there around Saturn?

How far from the earth is Pluto?

When did women start playing basketball?

Do we have any aliens?

How do blowfish blow up?

How do they shape paper into a square?

How does electricity reach something it needs to?

How do insects fly?

How many shapes are there to a cloud?

How can a basketball come down from such a skinny net?

How many bones does an elephant have?

How deep is the earth in feet and inches?

How many species of animals are there in the world?

I want to learn about the wars.

Could it be possible that there is life after death?

Are ghosts real?

Are psychics truly real?

How many kinds of Indian tribes are there?

How many gasses are in the sun?

What is a chemical, and how will it act with others?

How many grams are in a pound?

How many kinds of minerals are there?

What is the temperature in the center of the earth?

How big is Jupiter?

Why do deer like corn?

Why do fish have fins?

Why do horses have tails?

Why do bees have stingers?

Why do bunnies have paws?

Does Pluto have a magnetic core?

What is the best known black hole?

How much power does a black hole have to suck something in?

Is there life on Neptune?

What causes gravity to pull us down? *(asked four times)*

What makes gunpowder blow up?

Are there any other planets besides the nine we know? *(asked three times)*

How come you do not need aerodynamics in outer space?

Is it scientifically possible that there is actually life on other planets?

Is there any place on earth that doesn't have gravity? *(asked two times)*

Is Pluto the last planet? *(asked three times)*

Why is there friction on earth? *(asked three times)*

Is there friction on other planets?

How do lizards lose their tails?

Why do some frogs shed?

How come cheetahs can run really fast?

How fast does a cheetah's heart beat if runs one mile at 70 mph?

Why aren't a cheetah's claws retractable?

Why do football players wear air helmets? *(asked two times)*

What are air helmets?

Is there life on the moon?

Where do most marsupials live?

Is there life on Mars? *(asked nine times)*

Is there water on Mars?

I wonder how it feels when you are in space.

Why is there gravity in space?

Are there such things as UFOs? *(asked two times)*

How do scientists know that the sun will suck in the planets in five billion years?

How do they know that the Andromeda Galaxy and the Milky Way Galaxy will
    collide in six or seven billion years?

What is gravity?

Is a comet ever going to hit the earth?

What is the strongest animal in the world?

What is the biggest animal in the world?

Why doesn't everyone believe in Jesus, God, and why do they think the earth was made in a big explosion?

Why are clouds made?

Why does our blood look purple, but when we cut ourselves it is red? *(asked two times)*

How come when you are in space you float?

What are sharks attracted to?

When was the first light bulb invented?

How are clouds formed? *(asked four times)*

How come false gold isn't gold?

How come if I cut myself it hurts, but when we cut my hair it doesn't hurt?

How many dinosaurs were there?

Why did the continental drift happen, and what was it like then?

Why do sharks sleep while they swim?

How tiny are snowflakes?

How big is Ireland?

How do our vocal cords work?

What chemicals make volcanic acid?

What makes the sun shine?

How hard is Mt. St. Helens volcanic rock?

How many languages are there in the world?

Are cicadas poisonous?

Why are some animals cold blooded and some warm?

How come junk food tastes good?

How do they make houses?

How do airplanes fly?

How do planets stay circling the sun and not float away?

How do planets turn?

Why is the heat in lava so dangerous?

Why are there layers of dirt and clay under the ground, and how do they form?

Why do we have planets?

Why is our earth a sphere? *(asked two times)*

Why is the sky blue? *(asked two times)*

Why do we have animals?

Why do insects have six legs?

Why do we have plants?

Why is space so dark at night?

Why is electricity so important?

If a mosquito bites you and you have a virus, will the mosquito get the virus?

Why don't monkeys' nails get really long since they don't cut them?

What are fingernails made of?

What do plants eat, and how do they breathe?

What do worms eat?

Why do worms live underground?

Why does the sun sink?

How are hills made?

How are boats and cars made?

Why do bugs have hard shells over them?

What is the hardest mountain in the world to climb?

How did lakes and oceans form?

How do they make toothpaste?

How do volcanoes erupt?

How are mountains formed?

How hard are mountains?

Why does sugar make your stomach sick?

Fifth Grade

How long does the average dog live?

Why isn't the moon always round?

If you have a sickness, and a bug bites you, will it get that sickness?

If an animal eats a sick animal, will the first animal get sick?

What is the biggest dinosaur bone found to date, and where was it found?

Why are dogs called "man's best friend"?

Why are dogs and cats good pets?

How does a frog croak?

Why is the sky blue? *(asked seven times)*

We went to an outdoor concert this summer. The singers sounded good until after
dark, then they started getting an echo that made it difficult for them to sing.
Why did they get an echo after dark and not before? Why did they get an
echo at all?

How do street lights turn on and off at night and day?

How many legs does a centipede have?

Why are clouds white?

How far would you have to be from the sun before you burn?

Why when you look at a full moon are some spots dark and some light?

How does a ball bounce when it is just rubber and air? *(asked three times, mostly about basketballs)*

Why can't astronauts go to Saturn?

Is the sky really purple?

How long would it take to get to the moon and back? (asked two times)

How many bones are there in a baby seal?

Are chinchillas vegetarians?

Why are platypuses thought to be mammals?

How many Newtons are there in three tons?

Why did the dinosaurs become extinct?

Can you take two different cells and clone a person?

Could you make actual DNA strands?

With our technology today, can a person reach Mars?

How many hurt birds or mammals come into a zoo each day?

Why do clouds float and we don't?

Why does a 50-watt bulb in your room burn out faster than a 50-watt bulb in a fire station?

How long does it take to grow a rose?

How many different breeds of dogs are there?

Were the dinosaurs warm blooded?

How big is our solar system?

If there isn't a cloud in the sky, how do clouds form? *(asked three times)*

Why do the planets shine like stars?

Do the stars ever burn out?

Does each star have its own solar system?

Can mosquitoes tell us about dinosaurs?

Why do certain birds not have flight?

How long ago was the first machinery discovered?

How many plants die each day?

How many animals die each day?

Is it possible that there is life in this universe besides here on earth?

What chemical is the most flammable?

What is the most explosive chemical?

Is there life after death?

How many gasses are in the sun?

How does Michael Jordan jump so high if gravity pulls him down?

How do worms keep alive when in the earth?

Is fog clouds from the sky or does it naturally appear?

Scientists say that whales used to be land mammals and they had back legs, then they slowly turned into what they are now. My question is: why do they still have a part of these old legs?

How do you turn the sun's light into electricity?

Is there life on other planets? *(asked three times)*

Is there a planet "Cute"? If so, do the Moldmen and Grebarz really exist?

Why do butterflies like flowers?

When a monarch caterpillar changes from a caterpillar into a butterfly, what happens? It changes so much, and in so many ways, and in just a few days—but how?

What makes wind?

How do parts of our bodies work automatically without us thinking like the heart, breathing, pupils, dilating, etc.

How do clouds stay together? Why are some puffy and some wispy?

How do TV pictures and sound get into my TV?

What makes the world spin?

How does light travel from place to place?

How does the sun shine on the whole world?

What are clouds made of?

How many socks are made in an hour?

How long does it take for a butterfly to throw its life strand?

How many rocks are on the world? *(asked two times)*

How many plants are in the world?

Why does a conch shell sound like the ocean?

If molecules are all barely touching, why don't things fall apart?

How do bats stay in the air when it's dark outside?

How was food made?

How come the equator is warm?

How do planets stay up in space?

What do sloths eat?

How does light work?

How does water evaporate?

How do you hear a radio?

How does music get to the radio? *(asked two times)*

Why do some states have more storms than others?

Why don't birds get electrocuted by telephone wires when they land on them, but
  we do if we touch them?

Why can't koalas eat any other leaves besides the eucalyptus in Australia?

How do hippopotamus' faces turn red, and why?

How long would it take to get to Pluto from Washington, D.C.?

Why can't penguins fly?

How do magnets work?

Is there another galaxy?

How do we get heat from heaters?

How are a dog and a cat related?

When did the first man appear?

How were the planets formed? (asked two times)

How fast can a blue whale swim, and how big is it?

How fast can a dolphin swim?

Is a giraffe the tallest animal, and how tall is it?

How hot is the sun?

How can you call someone on the other side of the world?

What speed do you have to reach to get out of the gravitational pull into space?

What are the nine planets?

Why do fans shoot cool air? *(asked two times)*

Why do we eat food?

How do birds fly?

How can you break your eardrum with a Q-Tip?

How fast are sound waves?

What is our most needed planet? (The sun is a star, not a planet.)

Why do we have the Olympics?

How were rabbits formed?

Who invented the jokes of the world?

How fast does light go? *(asked two times)*

What rock is lead made from?

How do plants get their color?

What is light?

Where did water come from?

Why do we have snot?

How long does it take sound to travel from my house to Haslett (a town in Michigan)?

How many ticks does a clock make in an hour?

Why is there such a thing as an eclipse?

What do ants eat?

Why did the dinosaurs die?

What is leather made out of?

How come cats eyes glow in the dark?

How did the Grand Canyon form?

Why does California get the most earthquakes?

Does the ocean sink?

Why is there no gravity in space?

How can squirrels climb vertically?

Could any animal survive in space?

Why are people's eyes red in pictures?

What are rocks made out of?

How does sound travel?

How can the temperature rise?

How can light travel?

How can you hear birds outside?

Why do vibrations vibrate?

How can dolphins hear?

What does barking mean from a dog?

Do birds really talk or do they mimic?

Why are mosquitoes important?

Can dogs understand what we say?

Which is smarter, cats or dogs?

Could any animal, insect or reptile talk if they put their minds to it?

Why do scientists think there could only be life on planets we could live on?

What produces wind?

Why can't you see atoms if there are so many of them?

Why doesn't a comet just hit the earth and explode?

Why doesn't a disease like AIDS become airborne and kill everyone?

Why is the ocean salty?

How can we stay alive for 80 or 90 years, why not two?

How do you become deaf?

How do magnets stick to things?

Why is it that a butterfly and other flying bugs can just flap their wings to fly, and when we humans flap our hands and arms we can't fly?

How can light move faster than sound?

Why are plants alive?

How does lead write?

How are sound waves made?

How does medicine cure you?

How long does it take for sound to go from one person to another when they are standing five feet apart?

How many kinds of insects are there?

How fast does a ball have to go for you to hear it whoosh by you?

How long does it take a bird's egg to hatch?

How did water get into the ocean?

What is cement made of, and how is it made? How does it fall apart?

How far is it from the sun to Pluto?

Why do dogs have wet noses and toenails?

What is it that makes slugs sticky?

How do instruments make sound?

How does a TV work?

How does the remote control work?

How do videos work?

Why are babies so cute?

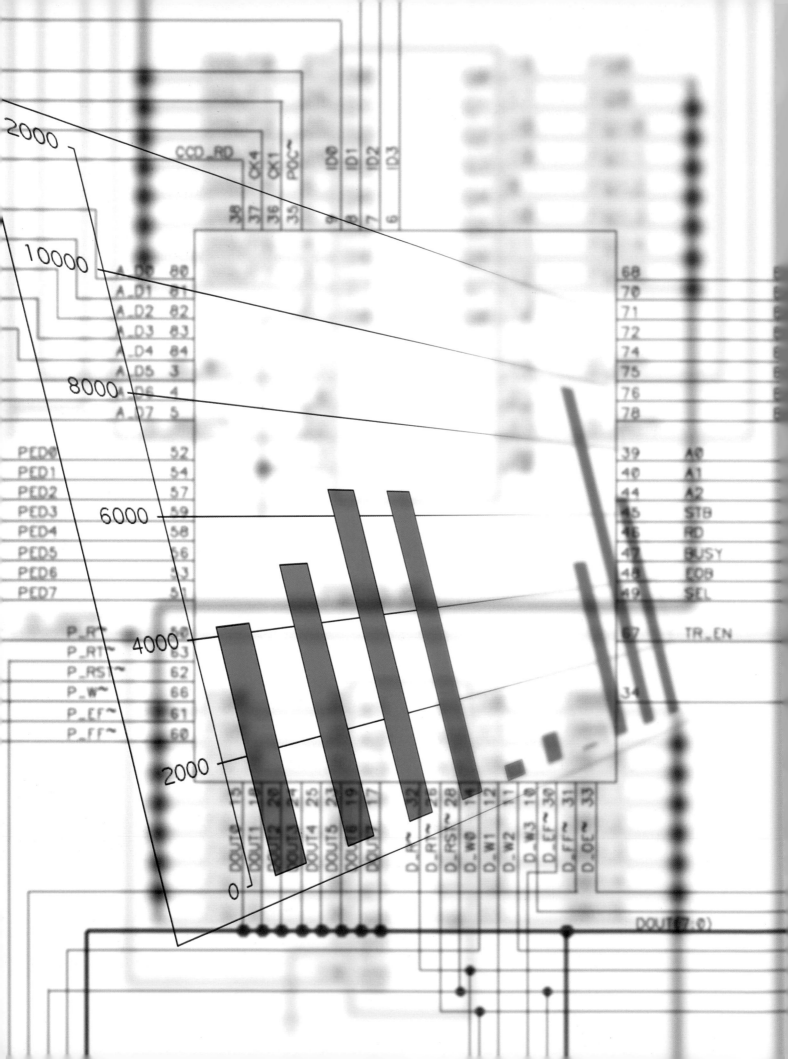

Sample Laboratory Notebook

Do Beans Grow Faster When Planted in Commercial Potting Soil, Forest Loam, or Sand?

3-7-98

Information about plants

- Plants need soil, air, light and water to grow.
- Plants use photosynthesis to produce energy. This means they use sunlight and carbon dioxide from the air to make their own "food." Photosynthesis occurs in the leaves and other green parts of the plant.
- Plants obtain minerals like nitrogen, potassium, and phosphorus from the soil.
- Plants obtain water from the soil. Water is drawn up by the roots and into the stems and leaves of the plant.
- Bean seeds should be planted one inch deep.

MODEL: The bean plants will grow fastest in potting soil because it is a rich soil (unlike sand) and does not contain weed seeds (like forest loam) that can compete with the bean plants for water and minerals.

Experimental consistency

1. Plant all beans one inch deep.

2. Use 8-oz. Styrofoam cups for all plants.

3. Fill the cups to the top ring with soil.

4. Place all cups on a tray on the kitchen counter. They will get the same amount of light and be grown at the same temperature.

5. Water all pots with the same volume of water.

6. Measure all seedlings at the same time of day each day (8:00 A.M.).

Controls

+ Beans planted in potting soil.

– No soil. Put three beans in a cup with water. Put four beans in a resealable plastic bag with a damp paper towel.

– No beans. Prepare one cup for each soil type that has no beans.

Replicates

Grow three beans in each soil type.

Materials

1. Thirteen 8-oz. Styrofoam cups.[1] Poke a hole in the bottoms of 12. Place a 2-inch square piece of paper towel in the bottom of each cup to keep the soil in the cup.

2. Potting soil (purchased)

3. Sand (purchased)

4. Forest loam (dug from under trees in back yard)

5. Bean seeds: Blue Lake 274 (NK Lawn & Garden)

6. Metal tray

7. Paper towels

8. Ruler

9. Resealable plastic sandwich bag

10. Water

11. Artificial light

Methods

Label cups. Poke holes in the bottoms of all cups except the no-soil control. Place paper towel squares in cups. Fill with soil to the top ring. Moisten soil thoroughly.

Allow pots to drain. Place pots on tray. Put one bean in each pot except negative controls. Push bean down about one inch. Cover with soil. Put three beans in the empty cup with water. Put three beans on moistened paper towel in resealable plastic bag.

   Beans were planted at 6:00 P.M. on March 7, 1998.

   Code for labeling: four pots per soil type. Label *A, B, C, D*.

- *ps* = potting soil (*psC* is the third pot with potting soil)
- *fl* = forest loam
- *s* = sand

3-10-98

Notes

- Giving the plants the same volume of water does not work. I want the soils to be equally damp. The three soils filter and retain water differently. Pouring water in the tray and letting the pots absorb the water maintains uniform dampness.
- The beans on the damp paper towel sprouted nicely. The beans in the cup of water turned to mush.

3-12-98

- First shoot appeared. *psC*

3-13-98

- First weed appeared. *flA*

3-15-98

- Only one bean has sprouted.

"One for the sparrow

One for the crow . . ."

Repeat experiment with more seeds.
Plant four seeds per cup.

Table A2.1. First Planting: 1 Plant (*psC*)

DATE	HEIGHT OF BEAN PLANT (INCHES)
3-16	2.0
3-17	5.0 (bean unfolded)
3-18	6.75
3-19	8.5
3-20	10.5
3-21	11.0
3-22	12.0

Second Planting

3-15-98

Plant four more beans around the edge of each cup—except negative control cups. Mark the location of each seed with a colored mark on the rim of the cup. See Figure A2.1. Start six new beans on a paper towel.

Code for labeling: four pots per soil type. This time, label *1, 2, 3, 4.*

- *ps3r:* potting soil, cup 3, near red mark
- *ps2b:* potting soil, cup 2 near blue mark, etc.
- *1–6:* no soil controls

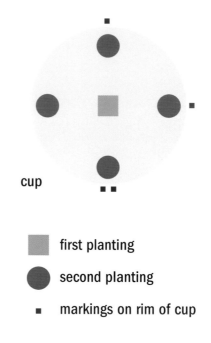

first planting

second planting

markings on rim of cup

Figure A2.1. Locations of Bean Seeds in the Cups.

Table A2.2. Appearance of Sprouts

DATE	DAYS AFTER PLANTING	PLANTS			
3-19	4	ps2			
3-20	5	ps1	fl2		
3-21	6	ps3	fl1		
3-22	7	ps2b	ps3b	ps3rr	
3-24	9	1			
3-25	10	ps1b	ps1r	4	6
3-26	11	ps3r	2		
3-28	13	s2			
3-29	14	s2b			

- For the no-soil controls, the appearance of sprouts was recorded when the shoot grew to be one inch long because other beans were planted about one inch below the surface of the soil. This may be an overestimation of sprouting time.
- The no-soil controls and their damp paper towels were transferred to a plastic tray when the bean plants grew too big for the plastic bag. Small pieces of damp paper towel were placed on top of the roots to keep the roots moist.
- The no-soil controls tend to have crooked stems because they cannot anchor themselves in the soil with their roots. The curving stems were measured by laying a piece of string along the stem then measuring the string.

Table A2.3. Bean Growth (height in inches of bean plants)

DATE	DAY	PS1	PS2	PS2B	PS3	PS3B	PS3RR	PS1B	PS1R	PS3R	fl2	fl1	S2	S2B	1	2	4	6
3-23	8	1	0.5	0.5	0.375	0.625	0.75				0.75							
3-24	9	3	0.875	1.25	1	1.5	2				2.25				1			
3-25	10	5	2.5	3	2.75	3.5	4.75				4	1			3.25		1.5	1.5
3-26	11	7	5	5.5	6.5	6	8	0.75	0.5		6.75	2.5			5.75	1	1.5	3
3-27	12	8	8.75	6.75	8.5	7.25	10	2.5	1.5	0.75	8.5	5.5			8.25	1.5	2	4.25
3-28	13	9.5	10	8.5	10	9	11.75	6.5	2.5	2.5	9.5	7.75			9	1.75	2	5.25
3-29	14	10	11.5	9.75	11.25	10	13	8.25	5	5	10.5	9.25			10	6.25	2.5	8.5
3-30	15	10.5	12.5	10.25	12	10.5	13.5	9.75	5.5	7.75	10.75	10.5		0.75	11	7.75	4	10.5
3-31	16	11	14	10.75	13	11	15.25	10.5	8.5	10.25	11.75	11.75		1.5	12.75	9.75	5.5	12
4-1	17	11.25	15	11	13	12	15	12	10	12	12	12	1.25	2	13	12	7.5	12.75
4-2	18	11.5	15	11	13.5	12.25	15	13	10.5	13.25	12.25	12.5	2	2.25	14.75	12.5	9	13.5
4-3	19	11.75	15	11.5	13.5	13.5	16.25	13.25	11.5	14.25	13.5	12.5	2.25	2.25	15.25	13	10	14.25
4-4	20	12	15.5	11.5	13.5	13.75	16.5	13.5	11.75	15	13.5	12.5	2.25	2.25	16	13.5	11	14.75
4-5	21	12.25	16.5	12	13.5	13	16.5	13.5	11.75	16	13.75	13	2.25	2.25	16	15.5	11.25	16
4-6	22	12.25	16.5	12	14.5	13	16.5	13.5	12	16	14	13	2	2	16	15	11.5	16
4-7	23	12.25	16.5	12	14.5	13	16.5	13.5	12	17	14.75	13	2	2	16	15	12	16

Graphs for these data are shown in Chapter 6, Figures 6.5, 6.6, 6.7, and 6.8.

Conclusions (from the second planting)

1. Nine of the 12 bean seeds planted in potting soil sprouted (75%). Two of the 12 seeds planted in forest loam sprouted (17%). Two of the 12 seeds planted in sand sprouted sprouted (17%). Four of the six beans germinated without soil sprouted (67%).

2. Beans planted in potting soil or forest loam or on a damp paper towel sprouted by the 11th day. Beans planted in sand sprouted later on the 13th and 14th days.

3. Beans planted in potting soil or forest loam and the no-soil controls grew to about the same height (12–17 inches). Beans planted in sand stopped growing when they were 2 inches tall.

4. Beans planted in potting soil or forest loam and the no-soil controls grew at the same rate because the slopes of the growth curves are similar. Beans planted in sand grew at similar or slightly slower rates.

5. The seed contains sufficient nutrients to support the bean plant until leaves develop and photosynthesis can occur because the seeds sprouted on damp paper towels grew as well as the seeds planted in the rich soils.

6. The two bean plants that grew in sand were malformed and never developed leaves.

7. Only two weeds grew in the forest loam. The experiment was done in March while there was still snow on the ground, so the weeds must have germinated from dormant seeds. Forest loam collected in the summer when many plants are flowering might produce more weeds because the soil would contain more weed seeds.

Additional questions and future experiments

What happened to the seeds that never sprouted?

Perform an "autopsy" on the unsprouted seeds. Dig into the soil with a popsicle stick and look for the missing seeds.

Autopsy results:

1. Bean seeds recovered from the forest loam were mushy, tan, and had spots of pale green mold.

2. Bean seeds recovered from the sand were pinkish-purple and mushy.

3. Not all planted beans could be recovered. Some must have decomposed during the three-week experiment.

Can the bean plants grown in sand be saved?

Carefully uproot the two bean plants from the sand, and gently wash the roots in tap water. Plant one bean plant in potting soil. Place the other in a plastic bag containing a damp paper towel.

Transplant results: (Observation period was one week.)

1. Neither bean plant grew after removal from the sand.

2. Neither bean plant developed leaves.

Why did the bean seeds planted in sand grow so poorly?

1. This sand was intended for use in children's sandboxes, so a chemical may have been added to the sand to inhibit weed growth.

2. Wet sand packs densely, and may not provide sufficient aeration for optimal seed germination. Note: potting soil contains vermiculite to increase soil aeration.

MODEL 1: The poor performance of bean seeds planted in sand was caused by a chemical that had been added to the sand to inhibit weed growth.

MODEL 2: The poor performance of bean seeds planted in sand was caused by inadequate soil aeration.

The two models can be tested with the following experiments:

- *Mixing Experiment:* How much sand can be mixed with potting soil before bean plant growth is retarded? Try 25% sand + 75% potting soil, 50% sand + 50% potting soil, 75% sand + 25% potting soil. Remember to include positive controls (potting soil) and negative controls (sand). The results of this experiment will not differentiate between the chemical and aeration models, but will demonstrate what percentage of sand is required to achieve the growth inhibition.

- *Vermiculite Experiment:* Does mixing 25% vermiculite with the sand or forest loam improve the performance of the bean plants? Positive controls: potting soil, and potting soil + 25% vermiculite. Negative controls: sand, and forest loam with no added vermiculite. This experiment tests the soil aeration model 2.

- *Water Quality Experiment:* Has the sand been treated with a chemical to inhibit weed growth? Is the chemical soluble in water? Will water poured through sand inhibit bean growth in beans grown in potting soil? Punch several holes in the bottom of a Styrofoam cup. Put a piece of paper towel over the holes and fill the cup with sand. Pour water into the sand and collect the water that flows through in a clean bowl. Use this water to water beans planted in potting soil. Positive controls: beans planted in potting soil and watered with fresh tap water. Negative controls: beans planted in sand and watered with fresh tap water. This experiment tests whether a water-soluble chemical has been added to the sand to inhibit weed growth, model 1. Note: if the chemical is not soluble in water, no effect will be observed.

N O T E

1. Next time, plant the seeds around the edges of clear plastic cups so the growing roots can be observed.